My Husband's Secret

by

Sonny B. Allen

Special thanks to Teri A. Black-Allen for her enthusiastic support in the publication of this book.

CONTENTS

PROLOGUE

San Francisco

December 2012

Sometimes I think of you and wonder if you ever think of me. Sometimes I'll remember how I fell in love with you and wonder if you ever really loved me. Author unknown

The first time she saw him she was captivated. Maybe it was the way he looked at her and smiled. Maybe it was his hair. Her mother told her once that only bad boys wore their hair long. Perhaps it was his accent, which she tried to discern rather than ask about it. She had only been in Bloomingdales department store for a few minutes and he immediately drew her attention. She was so intrigued by this boy toy stranger that she totally lost all sense of time and place. All she could focus on was him.

He looked magnificent in his blue Anton Laurent suit with the tiny pinstripes, paired

1

with a pink shirt and an olive green tie. His lean six-foot frame appeared to have been sculptured into the suit by an anonymous artist. She had a strong urge to caress him like a long lost lover. It was odd that a stranger who worked behind a department store counter affected her in that way, especially since her last relationship was a disaster. She was in no mood to meet someone new. This was different, though. Her reaction to this man was more than mere attraction.

She approached him with a question. "Can you help me pick out a necktie?" She wanted to buy a designer tie for her father. It was Christmas, and each year she gave her dad a new tie. In response, the stranger replied in his professional department store voice. "I would be happy to assist you in selecting one of our beautiful ties." He pointed to a display filled with expensive neckties. She noticed his eyebrows moved up and down when he spoke, as though an invisible puppeteer was hiding on the other side of his forehead. She found herself consumed by the stranger standing before her. He was strikingly handsome and looked too good to be true. Guys who looked the way he did were usually trouble, she thought.

Evan noticed Anna the moment she entered the store. He had a clear view of everyone who came in from the Market street entrance. Anna moved briskly, as if she had somewhere to be with no time to waste. He watched her long, athletic legs carry her quickly across the shiny floors of Bloomingdales. She moved like a catwalk model, shoulders back, spine straight and eyes focused straight ahead, in full command of her body. She was tall for a woman and wore a simple black skirt which clung to her curves. When she looked in his direction, he noticed her eyes were childlike, almond shaped, the color of chestnuts, with a hint of curiosity. Her hair was wavy with that chic unkempt look and the color of midnight.

Beautiful women frequented the store on a daily basis, but there was something unique about Anna. Evan was reminded of the philosopher Camus and how he described the way a woman's beauty can impact a man. "Beauty is unbearable, drives us to despair, offering us for a minute the glimpse of an eternity that we should like to stretch out over the whole of time." Camus's description was in perfect alignment with Evan's desires as he watched the elegant stranger heading his way. He waited for her to approach his counter as he thought in silence. *Who are you, pretty lady? Where are you from? I would certainly like to know more about you.* Once she was within earshot, he smiled warmly. She asked for help and he gladly offered to assist her.

"I'm looking for a designer necktie by the Italian designer Anatoli. Do you know him?" she asked.

"Yes I do, I wear his ties all the time. They are overpriced, but I get them at a big discount," he laughed. "My name is Evan, what's yours?"

"I'm Anna," she replied, extending her hand.

They shook hands and he listened carefully as she spoke in a low, velvety voice. He was reminded of those old time movie stars with the smoky sounding voices. Voices that reeked of sophistication and sexuality. They chatted about the necktie collection, travel, fashion and anything else that guaranteed they would stay in each other's presence awhile longer. The more they spoke, the more comfortable they became with each other. She was surprised by his friendliness and wondered whether this was a facade. Did he want her to buy a $150.00 necktie, or was it because he sensed the same attraction she did as they examined each other carefully?

Anna was content with the unspoken attraction when Evan unexpectedly offered to buy her a cup of coffee during his work break. A streak of excitement rushed through her body as she considered his offer. She had to be careful because she'd only met him ten minutes ago and this was San Francisco, where a lot of crazy things can happen. Her mouth responded involuntarily before her brain could process his offer.

"Yeah, that sounds nice, coffee would be great. By the way, will you be selling me a tie today?" she asked.

They both laughed, since it was obvious their mutual interest in each other seemed to override the reason she had come to Bloomingdales.

"Of course I will," he said, smiling.

Minutes later they sat in a large booth in the basement of the store not far from the exit door. The restaurant was dimly lit and Anna thought it was romantic. *I have never felt this comfortable with anyone I just met 30 minutes ago*, she thought, admiring Evan's boyish looks. Anna was curious as to why Evan approached her in the first place. Why had he offered to have coffee with someone he'd just met? She wondered how many times he had pulled this number with other young women in the past. Surely she was not the first.

Evan Bulon attended law school at the University of California at Berkeley. He was fortunate. His father, who lived in Europe, had covered all his law school expenses. But he enjoyed working at Bloomingdales, and the extra money came in handy. As he spoke, Anna couldn't help but gaze into his eyes. They looked honest, and he had the most beautiful skin she'd ever seen on a man. His complexion was very smooth and clear of any blemishes. She wondered whether he used those new skin products for men. His hair was coal black, which contrasted nicely against his hazel eyes. He was unfairly handsome and in all probability gay.

Everyone knew those beautiful young men in the department stores downtown were gay. Nonetheless, their conversation flowed easily and Anna felt as if she was talking to an old friend. She could not believe how intense the energy was between them. He was single, not dating anyone, and enjoyed fine wines and foreign movies. She found him fascinating the more she sat and listened to him.

He was born in Zurich, Switzerland. His parents moved to Paris when he was young and that was where he attended school. He spoke several languages and was very bright. Evan's parents divorced when he was a teenager and his mother relocated to Amsterdam, taking Evan with her. He was still close with both parents and loved them dearly. His father remarried and moved to Greece. He was an important businessman who ran a major research company. Anna, however, did not care where Evan was from because she knew she liked this guy. She decided if he was gay they could still be friends. She figured it was a winning proposition.

However, the more he talked about the places he had visited or lived, the more insecure she felt. Maybe it was because he seemed so worldly and sophisticated compared to her. She had a boring upbringing. But Anna quickly realized she was being silly, and Evan must have sensed how she was feeling because he began telling her about all the mistakes he'd made in his 28 years, as though he wanted her to know he was not to be envied. When she told him how impressed she was by him, he laughed out loud.

"Are you kidding? I'm working at a department store as a retail clerk selling overpriced luxury goods to people who don't need them," he joked.

She laughed and realized he was funny with a magnetic personality. He was soft spoken, intelligent, and most of all he seemed to really like her. Perhaps he wasn't gay after all, but he still seemed too good to be true.

Anna grew up in Mill Valley, just fifteen minutes north of San Francisco, right over the Golden Gate Bridge. The town was known as a mecca for creative types where musicians, artists, and writers abounded. There was a bohemian feel, yet it was one of the most expensive places to live in the country. Anna's father was a neurosurgeon at Stanford University Hospital, while her mother was a renowned patent attorney in Silicon Valley. She was the only child of Kent and Claire Cain. Their earlier attempts to have children resulted in two stillborn deaths. They continued trying until Anna was born on January 20, 1984. She had a typical upper middle class childhood. She was an excellent student and always made her parents proud. Anna was exactly what Claire and Kent Cain had hoped for. She had an independent nature and was curious about everything. Her love of technology began at age six, when her mother bought her a toy computer for Christmas. After she graduated from Stanford, Anna became a software engineer. She was almost always the only woman in her engineering classes during her college years, but she enjoyed the challenge and graduated in the top tier of her class. She worked for a major tech company in San Francisco, where she was on a fast track for promotion.

Driving home, Anna could not stop thinking about Evan. Her heart raced in anticipation of seeing him again. They'd agreed to take in a movie and dinner the following weekend. For Anna, Saturday could not come fast enough. She had already begun counting the hours until she would see him. She would have to survive another 110 hours before they met again.

Evan couldn't wait to see Anna the next weekend. He thought about all the things he wanted to share with her when they met again. He would tell her how much he loved Paris, and all the funny things he had experienced in Athens one summer. He would also tell her about the art gallery in Amsterdam where his mother's paintings hung. But most importantly, he would tell Anna how he felt about her. Even though she was still a stranger, he wanted her to let her know how important she was to him. The fact that they didn't know much about each other did not matter because the chemistry between them was undeniable. All his life, Evan had heard about how people feel when they really fall in love. He did not know whether this was love with Anna, but he knew the way she made him feel truly meant something. That was good enough for him.

Evan stared out his apartment window and watched the thick fog roll over the city as he thought only about Anna. How unreal it seemed to have met such a wonderful woman. He sensed that she was special and wonderful things would soon follow. He poured himself a gin and tonic and fell asleep with nothing on his mind but Anna.

"HELP ME! HELP ME!" Evan screamed, waking up in a cold sweat at 2:45 in the morning. He was short of breath and panic with fear. He bolted upright in bed, body trembling uncontrollably as perspiration dripped from his armpits and tears flowed down his face. He knew what was happening. Whenever he allowed his thoughts to wander into forbidden areas of his mind, he suffered a violent physical reaction. It was a physical defense mechanism, the result of the extreme fear that someone close to him might uncover the enigma that had haunted him his entire life. He took his medication to relax, as he did after every episode, and drifted back to sleep.

Over the next few months, Anna and Evan grew closer. Their relationship blossomed beyond either of their expectations. It was obvious to anyone who paid attention that the two of them were falling wildly in love. Evan desperately hoped this relationship would be different from the others, because he loved Anna so much. His past relationships were usually broken off after a brief period because they rarely extended beyond the kissing stage. His old girlfriends would leave him after a while, wondering what was wrong with him. Some thought he was gay since he never tried to make love to them. He knew that was not the case and if it was, it would be a minor problem compared to the true reason for his behavior.

But things would have to be different with Anna. She would become suspicious if he never made the effort to be intimate with her. She would wonder why nature hadn't taken its course between them. This would present unimaginable complications in a serious relationship with Anna. He felt helpless and confused because he had no answers to an impossible situation.

Evan sat quietly in Starbucks, anguishing over the reality of his dilemma. The more he thought about it, the more distressed he became. Clutching his head in agony, he screamed out for all to hear. "SOMEBODY HELP ME! WHAT AM I GOING TO DO?" The loudness of his voice reverberated throughout the store. Everyone stared at the handsome stranger who seemed to be having a nervous breakdown, or worse.

CHAPTER

1

Anna Cain was the happiest girl on the planet. Two days ago she was promoted to Vice-President of Software Development for Pallas Software, and the love of her life just bought two tickets to Paris to celebrate their wonderful relationship and her promotion. She would have never believed that shopping in Bloomingdales for her father's Christmas present would result in meeting the man of her dreams. They had dated for six months and were having the time of their lives. They spent weekends in Napa taking mud baths and drinking the finest of wines. Sometimes they would fly down to San Diego to spend weekends with Anna's friend Josie and her husband Roy. They would toast marshmallows and drink Grey Goose vodka while whale watching off the coast of Point Loma. She had never been this happy before with anyone at any time.

During the evenings the two of them would roughhouse like teenagers before bed until they were breathless. They spent a lot of time kissing and caressing in their private moments and their love grew stronger by the day. Anna was delighted that Evan never tried to pressure her into having sex. She'd had a few boyfriends in the past, but each one spent most of their time trying to get her into bed. She wanted to wait until marriage, which was difficult at her age. It was sometimes embarrassing to tell former boyfriends she was a virgin and wanted to wait until marriage. Their response was either disbelief, or they thought she was a lesbian.

Anna's family was a conservative Christian family. They strongly believed sex was reserved for marriage. Anna always thought it was odd that her parents chose to live in one of the most liberal areas of the country with their conservative beliefs. But it was never a problem because her parents were very accepting of people generally and did not believe it was their place to tell others how to live their lives.

Anna was very progressive in her thinking, but when it came to sex she agreed with her parents and had fought an ongoing battle within herself to remain celibate. She felt this was a way to honor her parents' wishes, but it was also something she believed in.

Since meeting Evan it had become very hard to keep her promise to remain a virgin. Her passion level rose with a vengeance each time he touched her. Evan never tried to go further than kissing, even though her body was ablaze with desire. She would marvel at his ability to control his passion. When she told Evan how she felt about sex before marriage, she held her breath in fear of what he might say. She was shocked and relieved that he totally agreed and told her not to worry because his love for her was strong and they had plenty of time for sex. She was ecstatic with his response, but wondered why he seemed almost euphoric when she told him about her being celibate. He looked relieved. *Is there something he's not telling me?* she wondered.

Other guys would usually get upset and soon be gone out of her life, but not Evan, he was truly special. There was something very different about him.

Anna was overjoyed about going to Paris. This would be her first trip to Europe and she wanted to do all the tourist things like visiting the Eiffel Tower and Notre Dame, and travel the Champs-Elysées. Evan gave her a crash course in basic French and she took a French cooking class for one week. He was amused at how serious she was in preparing for her first trip to Paris. He reminded her that he spoke French and she would be in good hands.

When they landed at Charles de Gaulle airport they were tired and only wanted to get to the hotel and go to bed. It was near midnight and the weather was cold and raining. They checked into the hotel and Anna spent the first hour in Paris staring out the window at one of the most fascinating cities in the world. Even though she was tired, she could not turn away from the view from her hotel window. Her imagination just took off thinking about all the movies and books she had read about the people and the culture of France. She was in Paris with the man she loved, and nothing could be better.

The next morning the weather was cool and clear. The sun shone off the Seine like a yellow jewel off in the distance. Paris looked like a panoramic postcard. She was excited to be in such a grand city as she prepared for a day of sightseeing. During the day they visited some of the most famous sites in the world. After a while she noticed Evan seemed quieter than normal, but she did not worry because she was sure he would tell her if something was wrong.

They were having coffee at a sidewalk cafe when Evan's cell phone rang. He stood and left Anna sitting at the table alone while he walked a few feet away to speak in private. She wondered who was he speaking with and why he felt the need to be alone. Was he trying to hide something from her? He returned minutes later with a frown on his face. She was sure something was not right.

"Is everything ok, Evan?"

"Yeah, I guess so."

"You guess so? What do you mean, sweetheart?"

"My father called from Athens. He will be in Paris tomorrow and wants to see me."

"That's great! I will get a chance to finally meet him."

"Yeah, but I must tell you what he's like before you do."

"What do you mean, honey?"

Evan told her his father had a controversial background. He had been under investigation by government authorities in Greece, France and Spain.

"Is he some type of criminal?"

"No, he is not a criminal. My dad is a brilliant businessman with many secrets. He told me once that he had done things he regrets, but in general he believes he has done tremendous good through his work."

"What does that mean?"

"Some of his business practices were considered unethical by some. But my dad feels his work is very important, if not revolutionary, and will eventually benefit all of mankind."

Anna did not know what to think about Evan's father. Evan seemed nervous and jittery when he discussed his father. She quickly changed the subject and he seemed pleased.

"Are you in the mood for one of my famous cocktails? she asked with a sly grin. "What cocktails?" he asked. "I know how to make the best cosmopolitans in the world. I will make you one using my secret ingredients."

Evan laughed aloud as Anna begin mixing her special concoction. Later that night after consuming at least four cosmopolitans each, they were bombed and hanging from the ceiling. They sat up until three in the morning enjoying Anna's homemade cosmopolitans and laughing uproariously while watching old episodes of the three stooges on french television.

They overslept and rushed to get to the airport the next morning. The freeway traffic was heavy and it took over two hours to reach the airport to pick up Evan's father. They were an hour late and his father sent several text messages to Evan asking where he was. Even though Evan explained about the heavy traffic, his dad was still upset.

"My dad is very impatient and in his mind, traffic problems are not his problem."

Anna was curious about Evan's dad. She only knew he was an important man who was very impatient and had a son she was in love with. Frederic Bulon did not look like she imagined him. He was shorter than Evan, but had the same hazel eyes. His gray hair was cut stylishly short and he looked athletic for a man his age. When he looked at Anna, her discomfort was palpable. He had a look in his eyes that made her feel he knew every secret she'd ever had. Anna observed him carefully. He moved slowly, like a prowling cat, yet never taking his eyes off her. When Evan introduced her to his father, he cracked a slight smile and said hello. She stood quietly as he examined her. There was an awkward pause until he spoke.

"Evan, your girlfriend is very pretty."

"Thanks, dad. Anna is great and we are very happy."

Evan had not seen his father in five years and they agreed to have dinner to celebrate being together again. Frederic made a reservation at one of the top restaurants in Paris called Arpege. He was able to get a reservation with one phone call to someone he knew in Paris with important connections. Anna and Evan did not question their good luck in getting a reservation and looked forward to dinner. During dinner Anna remained quiet as Frederick discussed his work. He said his company's research would benefit mankind, although he never said what exactly the research was. Anna felt like a student in a classroom listening to the wise professor discuss his work in rapt attention. In reality, she had become bored and was looking forward to her day trip tomorrow with Evan.

Frederic finally stopped talking and asked Evan how long had he and Anna been dating.

"We have been together about six months, dad."

"Six wonderful months!" Anna said as she inserted herself into the discussion.

Frederic asked Anna to tell him about her family. She began telling him about her dad's work as a neurosurgeon and her mother's as a patent attorney. He listened without interruption as Anna talked about college, California, her job and her views about a number of topics. Evan remained quiet and beamed with pride as he watched Anna deftly answer his father's questions while making it clear that she was someone with a good intellect.

Frederic suddenly interrupted Anna and asked her what her long term plans were. She began to elaborate on her career plans and he interrupted again. "I'm talking about your plans for my son. What is it you want from him?" The room was suddenly quiet and the atmosphere turned icy as Anna stared at Frederic. She was taken aback and confused by his question and his tone of voice. She felt as if she was being questioned by a prosecutor in a courtroom. Frederic was no longer smiling when he questioned her. His eyes narrowed and a scowl appeared across his face. He seemed highly agitated.

Evan interrupted, "Dad, why are you questioning Anna in that manner? You're speaking to her as if you were a cop or something. What is the deal with you, dad?" His voice rose in anger. Frederic stopped his questioning and apologized. "I'm sorry, I'm just looking out for my only son. There are a lot of woman who would love to get their hooks in my son because of my family's wealth and prestige."

Anna was speechless. She had never encountered anyone like Evan's father. The way he spoke to her made her uncomfortable. She saw something in his eyes that she did not recognize, and it was not good. She wondered what he meant by Evan's wealth. Was there more about Evan she did not know? When dinner was over, Anna gave Frederic an awkward kiss on the cheek good night, but she could not wait to leave the restaurant. The evening ended quietly and Evan and Anna returned to their hotel. Neither spoke during the cab ride back to the hotel.

Anna could not sleep. She felt sad and confused about Evan's father's behavior. She asked Evan about it and he told her not to worry, because it was nothing. He said she would have to get to know his dad and she would understand him better. "Anna, my dad is not a bad person." She could tell that it was important to him that she believed what he said about his father. She smiled and said ok, and they kissed good night. But in the quiet solitude of the dark bedroom, she knew something was not right.

The noise startled Anna from a deep sleep. She could not figure out where the loud voices were coming from until she realized Evan was no longer in bed. She heard the sound of his voice coming from the hallway. She pulled back the covers and slid slowly out of bed. She peeked down the hallway and saw him talking to someone on the desk phone. She watched silently as he begins screaming into the phone. His arms flailed wildly as he ranted and walked in circles like a mad man. His face twisted in rage and turning as red as a beet. Her heart raced with fear as Evan's voice became louder and louder. She wondered for a split second, who was this man?

"I TOLD YOU I LOVE HER AND IT'S NONE OF YOUR BUSINESS, DAD. YOU CANNOT CONTROL MY LIFE, SO PLEASE STOP IT! I DON'T GIVE A FUCK WHAT YOU THINK!"

He slammed the phone down so hard it fell to the floor with a loud clanking sound, hitting the marble floors with great force. Anna quickly moved back into the bedroom and got under the covers as if she had never left the room. She wondered what they were talking about and what was going on between the two of them. Evan returned to bed and was surprised to see Anna awake.

"I thought you were sleeping."

"I was, but the noise of your telephone conversation woke me up."

"I'm sorry honey, but I lost my temper with my dad."

"What's going on?"

"I don't want to discuss anything more tonight. I only want to go to bed, if you don't mind."

Anna was upset because he would not tell her anything. She felt she had a right to know. The atmosphere had become toxic since Frederic's arrival in Paris. Anna could feel his resentment towards her and could not figure out why. He seemed threatened by her relationship with Evan. There was something between Evan and his father that was not good.

Sunday morning in Paris was wonderful. It was a beautiful day and the tourist crowds were large and friendly. Anna and Evan visited Notre Dame and enjoyed the spectacle of visiting one of the most famous sites in the world. She was in a great mood and happy to be in Paris. She did her best to forget about the dinner with Evan's father last night, and the screaming match Evan had with his father on the telephone during the wee hours of the morning.

A few days later, Frederic was leaving Paris to return home. Anna pretended she was not feeling well as an excuse not to join Evan in taking his father to the airport. She was ashamed because she really did not want to see Frederic anytime soon and was too embarrassed to tell Evan. She was intimidated by Frederic during dinner at the restaurant a few nights ago and did not want to be in his presence again. Evan kissed her as he left for the airport and said he would be back soon. She did her best to try and figure out what happened at dinner a few nights ago. She wondered what could explain Frederic's behavior.

Evan called Anna from his car and told her he was taking her out for a special dinner on their last night in Paris. He told her how much he loved her and was convinced he could no longer go on in life without her. His words were so powerful that she fell to her knees quietly sobbing with emotion. Evan became concerned because there was only silence on the other end of the phone. "Anna, are you ok, sweetheart? Are you there? Is everything all right?"

She finally found the strength to respond. "YES DARLING! I'm the happiest woman on earth. This is so wonderful! I love you so much, Evan. Words are inadequate to describe the depth of my love for you, sweetheart."

The candlelight dinner at Lc Ciro was magnificent. Evan ordered the best wine on the list and a dozen roses, which arrived as soon as they took their seats. Anna could not believe what was happening. She truly loved Evan and had hopes for marriage, but not this soon. They had only dated for six and a half months. But her feelings for Evan were so strong she decided it did not matter if it was six months or six years; she loved this man more than words could express.

Evan looked handsome with his fresh haircut, Duvalier suit and a look in his eyes that exuded magic. Anna wore a special dress she'd bought especially for their last night in Paris. Evan thought the maroon colored dress made her look like a princess. The night was filled with hilarity as they drink the best wines and told dirty jokes. After a while all was quiet as they gazed into each other's eyes. He held her hand and in a low voice said, "I love you more than anything in the world, and I want you to be my wife. Will you?"

She always wondered what it would be like when her true love proposed, and now she knew. With tears rolling down her cheeks she said, "YES! I want to be your wife." The words left her lips like magic, like someone else was speaking through her body. It was surreal. They stood and kissed passionately in the middle of the restaurant floor. When they stopped, a couple nearby applauded. Anna's passion was overflowing like hot lava. She now knew she would have the man of her dreams and her full womanhood could finally be unveiled to the man she wanted to spend the rest of her life with. They both laughed because they agreed this entire scene could have been out of a 1950s movie with a couple of those old time movie stars like Katherine Hepburn and Rock Hudson from back in the day.

CHAPTER

2

" You're getting married? I can't believe it," exclaimed Madison 'Maddie' Phan, Anna's best friend and confidante. Madison and Anna had been best buddies since Montclair Elementary and had kept in touch throughout the years. Madison lived down the block from Anna growing up in Mill Valley. Her family was originally from Vietnam and owned a chain of successful restaurants throughout California. She was an excellent student, but she was also a rebel with a strong will and a very independent nature. She would tell Anna stories about how disappointed her parents were when she did what she wanted rather than follow their wishes. She was a high-strung, freewheeling 'wild child'.

Madison received an academic scholarship to Yale after high school. Instead, she decided to take a hiking trip with her 26-year-old boyfriend to Peru for six months. That was one of the reasons Anna loved Madison, because she was courageous and would do things that Anna would never have the courage to do. The two of them were considered uncool by the other kids. Anna was seen as a prude because she was celibate. Many of the other kids considered losing their virginity a badge of honor, but Anna did not. Madison was thought of as an oddball because she did not fit the typical Asian bookworm stereotype. She was more of a bohemian adventurer. Anna would joke that they were like two peas in a pod, destined to meet life head on. Anna listened as Madison babbled on with a million questions about her relationship with Evan.

"Who was he? Is he hot? When did he ask you to marry him? etc., etc. I knew you were dating some guy you met at Bloomingdales, but I had no idea it was this serious. Shit, girl! You are amazing. I want to hear all the dirty details and I know I will be in the wedding, RIGHT? Can I be your Maid of Honor?"

Anna could not stop laughing. Madison was so excited that Anna was unable to get in two words during the conversation. Madison finally calmed down and Anna told her she wanted her in the wedding. They talked for the next hour, with Anna filling in all the details and history of what happened over the past six months between her and Evan.

"I have never heard you speak this way Anna; you must really love this guy."

"I do, Maddie, more than you could ever know."

The voice on the other end of the phone went quiet. Anna could hear the sniffling and realized Madison was crying.

"I... I...I'm so happy for you, and I love you, Anna."

"I love you, Maddie, you are my oldest and dearest friend."

Madison was never one to dwell on anything too long and in the next minute she wanted to know all the details about the wedding. "Take it easy, home girl, not so fast," Anna laughed. "Evan and I haven't told our parents yet and we haven't really planned everything. The only thing we have done is choose a date."

"When is it?"

"June 12. I want to be a June bride just like my mother was."

When Anna finished talking with Madison, she burst into tears. The reality of what was about to happen rolled over her in a wave of emotion. She realized Madison was the first person she told she was getting married and the sound of her voice repeating those words was overwhelming. Anna told Evan about her conversation with Madison.

"When will I meet this Madison?" he asked. "You're always talking about her."

"Sweetheart, I have been too busy falling in love with you. My friends have been texting me nasty messages complaining about me not being around since I met you," she laughed.

They realized the long hours Anna put in at work and Evan's law school studies did not leave time for much more. They both agreed to find time for their friends. Anna realized neither of them had met the other's friends except on one or two rare occasions. They planned a small cocktail party at her parents' house in Mill Valley. Evan had only met Anna's parents once. He liked them and they were impressed with him. Anna was excited about all her friends finally meeting Evan. She was particularly looking forward to Evan meeting Madison, since she was her closest friend and would be her Maid of Honor.

Anna's parents' home was nestled in the hills of Mill Valley with magnificent views. One could see the San Francisco Bay and the Golden Gate Bridge from the veranda of their home. It was also a perfect occasion to announce their engagement. Anna was proud of her parents in their efforts to make sure everything went well for the party. They hired a jazz band that played on the patio, creating a fun-filled atmosphere. The guests were an eclectic group representing fields as diverse as technology, music and politics. It was a festive day and Anna was having the time of her life.

Madison arrived early with her new French beau Maurice. She immediately ran over to Anna and gave her a big hug. Evan stood and laughed as he read the expression on Anna's face as she mouthed the word HELP! as Madison almost squeezed the life out of Anna in her excitement. Once Madison calmed down she walked over to Evan and gave him the once over. After a few seconds she broke out in a big smile, turned to Anna and said, "You did well, girlfriend, he's hot!" They all howled with laughter.

Maurice had remained quiet, but when Madison commented on how hot Evan was he smiled and shook his head in agreement. Madison grabbed Maurice by the arm and introduced him to Anna and Evan.

"It's great to finally meet you, Anna. Madison talks about you all the time. I said to her a few days ago, I must meet this Anna, she must be special," Maurice said. Anna blushed with embarrassment after his comment.

Evan shook Maurice's hand and asked how long had he been in California and what kind of work he did. Maurice was an art consultant and a good ten years older than Madison. Evan and Maurice hit it off from the beginning. They were huge soccer fanatics and loved Les Bleus, one of the top teams in France. They talked about how much each of them enjoyed Paris. Madison was the only one who had not been to Europe before, and after a few glasses of wine and a lot of dancing topped off with the largest blunt Anna had ever seen, the four of them pledged they would all visit Paris together.

Later in the afternoon, Anna's father called her and Evan forward, and they walked slowly towards him holding hands. They stood in the middle of the patio surrounded by friends and family. Anna's mother hugged the two of them and asked Anna to tell everyone about her little surprise, which she had only shared with her parent's hours earlier. Anna announced to all in attendance that she and Evan would be getting married in June. There was loud, raucous cheering that could be heard over the entire valley below. The crowd was euphoric in expressing their happiness for Anna and Evan.

Anna was in heaven as she sat with the man she would marry along with her best friend as they looked out over the bay on a blissful afternoon. She thought about how happy she was and how things were so different in her life. She remembered some of the disastrous relationships she'd had in the past and wondered whether she had to experience those to learn to appreciate how special Evan was. Evan looked at his first true love with affection and excitement. He prayed that marrying her was the right thing to do.

Carmel by the Sea was one of the most beautiful locations in California. The beach and the view of the Pacific made it a particularly romantic place for a wedding. Anna could not believe how everything was falling into place. Her mother and Madison helped plan the wedding. One of the biggest surprises was when Evan's father called from Europe and said he would attend the wedding. Anna could see that Evan was happy about his father attending the wedding, in spite of the big argument they had in Paris. When he told Anna, she smiled to conceal her true feelings about Frederic. There was something about him that unnerved her.

The way he looked at her in Paris and the night she heard the screaming match between the two of them had left her puzzled and fearful for Evan. She was surprised he would be attending the wedding, because he'd made it clear he would not be visiting the U.S. as long as Evan was involved with someone that did not meet his approval. He had obviously changed his mind. Anna was apprehensive about Frederic attending the wedding, but she knew there was little she could do about it. She tried to eliminate any thoughts about her future father-in-law and looked forward to the most exciting day of her life.

The months passed quickly and June 12 was a beautiful day for a wedding. Anna stood on the balcony of the chapel and stared at the guests below who were arriving in groups of ten or more. The air was filled with excitement and anticipation as the time for the ceremony approached. During a moment of quiet reflection, it occurred to Anna. *All these people are here to wish Evan and I good fortune as man and wife.* She was soon in tears as the new reality of her life sunk in.

The chapel grounds were a flurry of activity as people and cars jostled for space. The traffic was bumper to bumper down Ocean Avenue which was the major road that led into Carmel by the Sea. Guests had arrived from every corner for the wedding. Anna peeked out of the guest house window at the beautiful landscaped grounds where the ceremony would be held. It was a breathtaking sight. The blue ocean glistened in the distance as a thin whiff of fog covered the beach, where curious surfers and beach bums stared at the arriving guests in their tuxedos and gowns for the ceremony. Eucalyptus trees lined the walkway among the sandy trails and small private coves that dotted the grounds. The valet service was staffed by young men who looked like GQ models in their black suits and red bow ties. They rushed around like mad men, quickly taking the car keys from the hands of each arriving guest and parking the many expensive cars in locations surrounding the grounds.

Anna and her five bridesmaids sat in the guest house lounge drinking champagne as they tried to calm their nerves before the ceremony. They held rehearsals so everyone would know what their roles were. There was a singer from the San Francisco Opera who would serenade the bride and groom during the ceremony. Anna's mother was going to make a short speech about the importance of families coming together. The band that had played at her parents' home in Mill Valley had been hired to play for the wedding. Everyone was in a cheerful mood. The atmosphere was filled with a mixture of nervous energy and anticipation. Anna seemed to be the most relaxed of all. She had been waiting for this moment all her life.

Madison spent a lot of time crying and redoing her makeup after each crying session. She would later roll a fat joint of marijuana to relax. Anna could only laugh when she stared at Madison with her red eyes and mascara running down her face. She was a mess. Anna stopped laughing for a minute and took Madison out for a short walk behind the guest house to help calm her down. They sat on a bench and inhaled the cool ocean air. It seemed to relax Madison and she apologized for being a distraction. Anna told her not to worry and to have fun during the ceremony. Madison confided to Anna that she felt a deep sense of loss now that she was getting married. Anna listened as Madison spoke in an unusually soft voice.

"I feel kind of lost in a weird way, Anna. I have known you all my life and now you're leaving me. I know we still be friends, but it will not be the same. I feel as if I'm losing a family member." Madison was an only child and Anna was the closest thing she had to a sibling.

"Maddie, we will always be close friends. I have told you a thousand times you are my little sister and we will always be close, regardless of what happens. I have one thing I want you to do Maddie." "What?" "Stop your goddamn crying!" They laughed out loud and went back into the guest house after Madison promised she would stop crying.

Anna was on cloud nine. One of the highlights of today, besides her wedding, was to finally meet Evan's mother in person. They had developed a bond and respect for each other during their long distance phone conversations and Skype sessions during the months leading up to the wedding. Anna admired Else because she was her own woman. She was a successful artist, studied theater in Vienna and sold a successful business she started when she was younger. She also had a quirky personality Anna enjoyed. They would have conversations that would leave Anna screaming in laughter, usually after some bawdy joke. Although she had never met her in person, she felt a certain warmth and familiarity with Else.

Everyone became quiet as the time for the ceremony approached. Even the noise from the ocean surf seemed to have become quiet as everyone waited for Mendelssohn's Wedding March to begin. The music started as Anna and her bridesmaids moved into position to walk along the grass covered path that led into the chapel. She glanced back at her five bridesmaids as each of them beamed with excitement, their eyes moist with emotion. Anna took a quick glance at Madison, who seemed to be unusually relaxed. Anna figured she must have taken a big toke off a joint right before the ceremony. She knew she was right when she caught Madison reaching into her small silk lined purse for a large Snickers bar that she inhaled in what seemed like 30 seconds. Anna could not help but laugh.

Evan and his groomsmen looked elegant in their pinstriped tuxedoes. He was a little nervous, but very happy as he looked out over the audience and saw his parents sitting in the front row in the small wooden chairs that lined the walkway to the chapel dais.

His mother Else was striking in appearance. She wore a navy blue dress with a large red hat covering her head and a white peacock feather extending from the brim of her hat. She sat with her legs crossed, looking surprised at the number of people in attendance at the wedding of her son. She waved and smiled at people as they entered the chapel. A few seats down he saw his father Frederic, who was sitting with a woman he had never seen before. It occurred to him that this was the first time the three of them had been together in the same building for many years.

He remembered the three of them sitting around the fireplace one Christmas Eve when he was a small boy. For some reason, with both parents present, his mind harkened back to those days and a feeling of serenity welled up inside of him. He took it as a sign he was doing the right thing by marrying Anna. Maybe this would be the start of something new and a bright future for everyone in the family, he thought.

The ceremony was short and sweet. The minister said a few words. They pledged their love and life to each other and the rings were exchanged as they repeated the vows they had written together a few days before. They did not want the ceremony to turn into some sort of big production. They wanted the focus to be on the birth of a new life for the two people that everyone came to support and show their love for.

The reception was wild and a lot of fun. The song 'Celebrate' by Kool and the Gang blared out from the speakers behind the trees that surrounded the grounds. Somebody decided it was cool to hide the speakers and add to the magic of the event. The guest wondered where the music originated from as they danced to the most popular wedding reception tune in the world. Anna and Evan danced and shook their booty's until they were drenched in perspiration. Anna was no Janet Jackson, but she could shake it like no other on this particular day. She laughed as Evan's dance movements reminded her of someone having a seizure, with his wild flailing arms and jumping up and down like he was riding a pogo stick. She stopped laughing enough to ask him over the loud music, "Where did you learn to dance, homeboy?"

"I watched a YouTube clip last night on how to be a funky dancer at weddings," he said.

Anna screamed with laughter. "Oh my God! I cannot believe you did that." He grinned and simply shrugged his shoulders and continued dancing as she tried to control her laughter at her new husband, who was the worst dancer she had ever seen. *I now know he's not perfect,* she giggled.

Anna was nervous as Frederic embraced her. He gave her a peck on her right cheek as he whispered in her ear, "Welcome to the family." She smiled and thanked him while looking into his face with eyes that betrayed the words from his mouth. He was traveling with a well-dressed older woman who stood out from the other guests in appearance. She had a sculpted figure with an extremely small waist, much like a fashion model. She was beautiful with grey eyes and a youthful appearance. Her face was diamond shaped with high cheek bones. She must have been in her late sixties, but looking at her you would never have known it. She wore a suit that Anna had seen in the best boutiques in Europe and was dressed entirely in black and red, with a small red silk scarf tastefully tied around her neck. She was no doubt from Europe, with a strong fashion sense. She walked slowly up to Anna and introduced herself.

"Congratulations, Anna, I have been dying to meet you. Frederic told me how wonderful a girl you are. My name is Simone and I'm from Athens. I hope we have time to get to know each other better," she said as she leaned forward and kissed Anna on both cheeks in the European custom. Anna thanked her and gave her an awkward hug. Simone and Frederic walked over to Evan to extend their congratulations in the crowded chapel. Throughout the afternoon Anna could sense Simone's strong presence. Simone stood about 10 feet away among a small group, chatting. But each time Anna looked in that direction, Simone was staring at her intently, and she wondered why. Anna also wondered where Frederic's wife was, since he was remarried. She would not dare ask, but one had to wonder.

During the reception Anna made a beeline
for Else. She was just like Anna thought she
would be. She was tall, with Nordic features.
Her skin was fair with short brown hair and
eyes that reminded Anna of large black
buttons. Her eyebrows were bushy for a woman
and she had a cleft chin with a slight
resemblance to the actress Glenn Close. A sort
of beauty that was hard to define. She seemed
to have a permanent smile on her face, even
when she was not smiling. There was
something about her spirit that Anna found
special. It was an intangible sensation one
might get after seeing an old friend that you
have not seen in many years. Although she'd
only met Else in person an hour earlier. They
talked about everything from music to art. She
invited Anna to Amsterdam and she promised
to take Anna all over the place if she ever
visited there. Spending time with Else was like
hanging out with your best girlfriend. She was
kind and full of fun. Anna had never met an
older person like Else. She was so refreshingly
different from her ex-husband, Frederic. Anna

wondered how two people who were so different could have been married.

Anna and Else were having a great time laughing and enjoying each other's company. Else looked over at a small group of people chatting and asked Anna if she knew one of the guests among the group. "Who are you talking about, Else?"

"That little man in the brown suit wearing two left shoes." Anna looked over at the man standing nearby drinking champagne. He was actually wearing two left shoes. They both screamed in laughter. The champagne they were drinking probably made it funnier than it was, but they were laughing so hard that other guests walked over, curious about what they were discussing that caused the loud laughter. They all wanted to be in on the joke. After a while Anna and Else had a small group surrounding them and Anna enjoyed watching Else entertain her guests with witty stories and dirty jokes. They never told anyone what they were laughing about.

Later they took a short walk along the sandy pathway that led to the beach. The quirky smile and glow seemed to leave Else's face as her conversation took on a more sober note. Anna noticed Else had worry wrinkles spreading across her brow. The tone of her voice changed as she lowered it before she spoke and looked directly at Anna.

"Anna, I love my son more than life itself. He is a sweet boy with a good heart. There will be times that you will not understand certain things about him, but believe me, his love for you is genuine. When I was pregnant with Evan, there were serious medical complications that we thought would result in me losing my baby. His father is a proud, arrogant man who believed he had all the answers and was not going to allow any illness to take the life of his one and only son. My husband's best friend was a man named Dr. Jamie Heinz. Jamie treated me during my pregnancy using a never before tried medical experiment. Later, my medical problems disappeared and we had a healthy baby boy.

"But when Evan became a young man he learned he would have to face unusual challenges. I would only ask you to love and support him as long as my son exists on this plane."

"What do you mean by that statement, Else?" She did not respond to Anna's question. She quickly changed the subject and broke into laughter, asking Anna if she had heard the joke about the midget who visited a whorehouse for the first time. Anna was confused and did not understand why Else would change the subject from her son to one of her silly dirty jokes. She wondered whether Else was trying to hide something about Evan.

Anna and Evan had been married for a year and some things had changed. They initially agreed not to give up their apartments in San Francisco. They liked the idea of living between two places, although the majority of the time was spent at Anna's place since it was larger. Evan had moved all his belongings there, but maintained the lease at his old apartment. They agreed that it was time to get serious about trying to buy a home. They had an appointment with a real estate agent and began looking for a house. They agreed to give up their apartments and buy a place together, since it would represent a new beginning for them. Anna was excited about the search for the new house and was lucky that her parents helped with the down payment.

After a while they found a beautiful condo in the East Bay town of Albany. Anna loved the place because of the neighborhood, its access to San Francisco, and most of all it looked and felt like an all American town with tree-lined streets, beautiful parks and great weather. Somewhere in the back of her mind, she imagined having kids who could grow up in a town like Albany. They would ride their bikes down the neighborhood streets, play in the park and live an idyllic life. But the reality of what was happening between her and Evan rudely interrupted those thoughts like a nosey neighbor who decided to stop by unannounced.

Evan had become secretive and he would still have shouting matches with his father over the phone. He would never share with her what was happening that would cause him to become so angry. Whenever Frederic would call, Evan would leave the room so Anna could not overhear their conversations. *We are now man and wife. Why does he hide his conversations with his father, and what is it that causes him to become so angry?* she wondered. She had no answers to those questions. She was becoming accustomed to the routine between Evan and his father, but there was something else that bothered her.

After one year, they still had not consummated their marriage. Each time she attempted to get intimate with Evan, he had a reason not to do so. She was totally baffled by his behavior. They had several conversations about it and each time it would result in a fight. He would become highly agitated and begin yelling at her for putting too much pressure on him. His famous words were "everything in good time," which basically meant leave me alone. She had no experience with this and was totally lost. Anna decided she would seek outside help and mentioned it to Evan.

When she mentioned getting outside help for his intimacy problem, he suddenly changed his mind. He told her that he had been thinking about the whole situation and she was right. Certain things were expected in a marriage and he had not held up his end of the bargain. He told her to prepare herself for a special night and he would fulfill all her intimate desires. Anna was shocked. "What do you mean, a special night?" she asked.

"Stop asking questions, honey, just make sure you are prepared for a night of raw passion when I come home." He went out to buy his favorite pizza and said he would return soon. She laughed and said ok. He left quickly and with a sly smile, looked back at her and said, "Be ready tonight, baby girl." *What happened to him?* she wondered. Why the big change? She took his advice and looked forward to her special night. Maybe he'd come to his senses, or he was finally horny, she giggled.

CHAPTER

3

Anna never thought she would spend $500.00 at Victoria's Secret. She purchased everything from expensive negligee sets to a chocolate dildo as she prepared for her special night. She read numerous articles on the different uses for oils, lotions, and other things that would enhance her first sexual experience. She even bought a few rubber toys. She was determined to make this night one she would never forget. She had been waiting for a long time and she was going to take advantage of every minute. She had no idea of what to do with most of the stuff she bought, so she practiced on herself before Evan returned home. She wanted his warm body next to hers so she could become a real woman and allow the years of pent up desire and frustration to escape her passion starved body.

Anna prepared by taking a long hot bubble bath. She poured exotic oils from India in her bath water that smelled like roses and soap like vanilla. She used her Swedish sponge and slowly cleansed her body. She rubbed lotion on her body from head to toe. The woman at the store said it contained an element that would drive a man crazy with passion once he smelled the odor of her skin. She completed the ritual with Nuru oil that she rubbed between her inner thighs. She became aroused thinking about their bodies finally becoming one as they descended into the throes of intense passion.

She waited anxiously for Evan to return home. He had been gone over two hours without a word and had not answered his cell phone as Annie waited and almost fell asleep. She was beginning to seriously worry about his whereabouts when he walked through the door with a silly grin on his face. "Where have you been, honey?" she asked. He said something about running into a law school buddy at the pizza parlor and they got lost in conversation and the time got away from him. He grabbed her and gave her a big wet kiss as he continued apologizing. Although she was a little angry with him, when he kissed her, the passion in her loins began to rise with a vengeance. She'd spent the last few hours imagining what surprises this night would hold for her. *I have waited 28 years for this night and I will not let my irritation with Evan foul things up.*

"Sweetheart, I need to take a quick shower before we go to the bedroom," Evan said. Anna had been waiting all evening for his return and she was not excited about waiting any longer for him to take a shower. But she wanted everything to go right. She sighed heavily and waited. She got into the bed and slid under the covers, then removed her new negligee and waited for her husband. She looked up at the ceiling and reminisced about how her life had changed for the better. She had a great career and a man that she loved more than anything, and now she was going to finally consummate her marriage with her life partner. Passionate thoughts filled her head when a loud scream broke her concentration and startled her. "Oh shit! it hurts!" The sound of Evan's yell boomed throughout the house. Anna sprang out of the bed onto the plush carpet, running like a frightened deer as she raced towards the bathroom.

Wild thoughts rushed through her mind in the seconds it took her to reach the bathroom. *Was he having a heart attack? Had someone broken into the building and attacked him?* She slammed open the bathroom door in a state of panic to find Evan sprawled on the floor holding his back, his faced twisted in pain and agony. She quickly dropped to her knees and held him by his shoulders

"What happened, Evan? Oh my God! Are you ok?"

"I slipped on the wet floor and hurt my back. I think I've wrenched it."

"I'm going to call Kaiser Emergency Room."

"No, Anna! Just help me get up off the floor."

Anna tried to lift him from the floor to no avail. He was too heavy.

"We should call the doctor, Evan," she cried.

"NO! Don't call the doctor, just help me to get up on my feet."

"I can't lift you, you're too heavy."

Anna's head was spinning. On the most important night of her life, her naked husband was soaking wet lying on the floor writhing in pain and barking at her not to call for help. She was scared and confused and did not know what to do. After a while he quieted down and asked for Tylenol. She gave him several tablets and covered him with a large red beach towel. She laid on the steamy wet floor next to Evan as he winced in pain. She could not help but note the irony of the message written on the big red beach towel covering his torso. In large white lettering, the words, 'Have a Nice Day' were scrawled across the length of the towel.

Life is so weird, she thought, not knowing whether to laugh or cry. After an hour or so he said he was feeling better and told her to go to bed and he would be fine. She refused. "No, I'm going to stay with you." She sat in a lotus position on the floor cradling him like a child. He fell asleep after a while.

During the night he was able to walk back to the bedroom with Anna's help. She supported him as he walked slowly and uncomfortably. She could not understand why he would not allow her to call for help. The way he screamed in pain was shocking, yet the way he barked out orders to her not to call 911 seemed strange. *Why would someone do that if they were in severe pain?* she wondered silently. She laid awake all night staring at the ceiling while Evan slept like a baby.

Before daybreak, she felt him moving next to her and realized he was getting out of the bed. She watched him carefully slide from under the covers out of bed under his own power and walk normally towards the bathroom in the barely lit room. He moved stealthily, as if it was trying to sneak out of the bed without her noticing. He showed no signs of discomfort or pain and moved as if nothing had ever happened last night in the bathroom. He moved like a finely tuned athlete as he bounced across the floor to the bathroom with almost a skip in his step as she stared in silent amazement. *What a crazy night this was, and what in the hell is going on with Evan?* she wondered.

Thankfully, her sense of humor was intact as she giggled about the crazy situation. She could never have imagined her special night would be like this and that she would still be a virgin. She didn't know whether to laugh or cry at the ridiculous situation.

At breakfast the next morning, Evan seemed fine. He was in a good mood and was planning a trip to the Wax Museum. Anna sat quietly, trying to understand her husband and his odd behavior.

"Honey, how about driving over to Walnut Creek for dinner after we leave the museum? I heard that the food at Rivoli's is unbelievable, you want to go?" he asked.

She smiled and shook her head in agreement. Sitting across the table from her husband, she watched him wolf down pancakes and a large glass of milk. He laughed when he saw his reflection in the mirror with the big milk mustache covering his top lip. Anna did not laugh as he looked at her like a 12-year-old boy proud of his new milk mustache. There was never any discussion about last night. He never mentioned his back and the pain he suffered lying on the bathroom floor. It was almost like it never happened.

Evan's behavior changed over the next few months. After dinner each night he would go to bed early and alone. He would leave Anna watching movies or surfing the internet. When she tried to snuggle next to him in the bed wearing one of her new negligees, he would pretend to be asleep or pull away from her, or sometimes he would complain about being tired or having a headache. He seemed oddly cold and distant. Anna worried that it was her fault he was not physically attracted to her. She could not figure out what she was doing wrong. She followed all the lovemaking instructions she gathered from books and the internet. She did all the things that were supposed to make a man want her desperately. She even called Madison seeking advice. She was sure it was something that she was not doing that explained his behavior. But she was confused about how his behavior had changed. Before they were married, they both would become highly aroused as they made out. Maybe because they knew they were not going to go all the way, the excitement was more intense. She wondered what had happened. They were now married and he was a totally different person when it came to intimacy. The next morning on her way to work, her cell phone rang.

"Hey home girl, what's up?"

"I've had better days, Maddie."

"You don't sound like a new bride with stars in her eyes anymore."

"I know, I'm confused and worried."

"About what?"

"Evan seems to have lost all interest in me. It's as if once we said I do to each other during the wedding ceremony, he turned into an entirely different human being when it comes to intimacy."

"What do you mean, Anna?"

"He's fine during the day. We still enjoy each other's company and we have fun visiting museums, romantic dinners, movies, etc. But once we get home, everything changes when it comes to the bedroom. He treats me like a stranger. I sense no passion with him. He won't touch me in bed."

"Maybe you have cooties," she said in a burst of laughter.

Madison seemed to find humor in everything, that's how she was. Anna laughed at her comment even though she was not in a humorous mood.

"I'm sorry Anna, I am only trying to lighten the mood. Sometimes you have to be creative in getting a man's attention sexually; maybe he is one of those guys. Have you tried different things to lure him to bed?"

"I can't lure him anywhere. It takes two to tango, and Evan is just not interested for some reason. I have all kinds of kinky toys, oils, lotions; you name it, I got it. I even took one of those stupid belly dancing classes thinking the dance movements would entice him. The only thing I got was a bad case of carpet burn as I bumped and grinded on the bedroom floor while he fell asleep."

"Holy shit, Anna! do you think Evan is gay?"

"I don't think so, because I have seen him aroused when I walk around during the day in shorts or nighties. He will stare at me as if I'm a piece of fresh meat. But in the bed he's not there, even though I sense he wants me."

"You guys should go away where you can have a serious conversation about your relationship and just be honest with each other. A quiet place without interruption. Just the two of you and the four walls."

"That sounds like a good idea, but I'm not sure what's going on with him. I want to be happy, Maddie. I have waited my whole life for this moment and I don't understand what's happening."

"I got a feeling things will get better Anna, just hang in there."

"Yeah, maybe."

"Love ya, Anna, bye."

"Bye, Maddie, love ya too."

Anna was losing patience with Evan. She'd heard all the excuses for his behavior. It was time to confront him and figure out what was wrong.

She told Evan she wanted to go away for a few days to Bodega Bay.

"Why do we need to go to Bodega Bay? What will we do there?" he asked.

"I will tell you when we get there later this week." He looked puzzled, but agreed to go. He stared at her closely, eyebrows furrowed with worry wrinkles across his forehead.

She was beginning to feel strange and embarrassed about the whole situation. Consummation was supposed to be the part of a marriage that endeared a woman to her husband forever. An act where husband and wife give and receive one another and become literally "one flesh" which unites them for life in the eyes of God. But what do you do when your spouse is not interested? She would have never dreamed of spending this much time on something like this, and she certainly had not anticipated this would be a problem.

Before they were married, Evan would get heated up whenever she kissed or caressed him. *My God! maybe it's me and not Evan. Could it be that now that we are married, he is falling out of love with me?* Anna thought. Her friend Phil Jones once told her that some men really enjoy the chase, but once they capture the prey they lose interest. *What am I? A fucking rabbit he had fun trying to catch, but once he did, he moves on? I can't wait to discuss this with him when we are in Bodega Bay.*

CHAPTER

4

The Lovers Cove Inn sat overlooking the luminous Sonoma Coast. It offered an excellent retreat experience with unparalleled views of the Pacific and rooms with cozy fireplaces, decks and spa tubs since 1963. Anna did not finish reading the advertising piece she received in the mail about the place they would be seeking a getaway at Bodega Bay. *Why should I read this crap? I'm not going there to enjoy cozy fireplaces or spa tubs. I'm going to find out what is wrong with this man I married and love desperately.* She was surprised at the rising anger she felt whenever she tried to understand what was happening between her and Evan. She felt like a child who was being punished and ostracized for no apparent reason. *It was not supposed to be like this*, she thought.

Anna sensed Evan did not really buy into the idea of getting away for a private retreat to discuss their relationship. He began making negative comments about whether it was really necessary that they drive up to Bodega Bay to talk about their marriage. She felt he was considering changing his mind about going, even though he had agreed to go earlier. She was getting angry and frustrated, but she did not respond to the smart ass comments he made earlier during the day. When he said he thought it was stupid for them to go to Bodega Bay to discuss their relationship, Anna lost it. Before she realized it, she was screaming at the top of her voice at Evan. "WHAT IN THE FUCK ARE YOU TALKING ABOUT BUDDY? We have been married over a year and you have not acted like a real man, if you know what I mean. I have tolerated your bullshit long enough and if you want this marriage to work, you had better have your bags packed and be ready to go tomorrow morning, because I'm going with you or without you."

The room was suddenly silent as Evan stared at Anna. He looked as if he had just seen a ghost. His eyes were as big as saucers and his face seemed to be drained of blood. Anna was also surprised at her outburst. It was not like her to yell and scream at someone that way, especially someone she loved. She began to feel sickly, so she took Tylenol and went to bed. She knew that the frustration she felt hid a volcano of emotion that had overflowed, and Evan received it full force.

She prepared breakfast the next morning as Evan packed his bags for the trip to Bodega Bay. Neither had spoken to each other and they slept in separate rooms the night before. It was a beautiful day as they drove up the Sonoma Coast towards their destination. Anna was driving, which was unusual since Evan usually drove. Anna's foot was heavy as she pushed the accelerator to the floor and drove past the speed limit sign along highway 101 headed north. The large black numbers on the road sign read speed limit 65 mph. Evan looked at the speedometer and noticed they were moving between 85-90 miles per hour. He was concerned because the road was a narrow mountain road with sharp curves. He was about to caution her about driving too fast when a large deer sprinted in front of the car out of nowhere. "LOOK OUT, ANNA!" he yelled.

She steered the car to the right, trying to avoid the deer. "Jesus Christ!" Anna screamed as the brakes screeched and the car swerved and rolled down a 20-foot embankment. They screamed as the car raced down the bumpy hill over the rocks and heavy brush that covered the hillside. They were thrown around the car like rag dolls even with their seat belts on. Evan felt his head hit the car's roof as he was thrown towards the dash. Anna could not control her arms to brace herself as the car finally stopped rolling, coming to a rest on a flat gravel bed. They both survived the violent ride down the embankment. They were surprised they were not seriously injured and the car was not severely damaged. Evan looked at Anna, who had tears in her eyes.

"Anna! Are you ok?" he asked. Her blouse was torn, hair disheveled and she was breathing heavily. He could see the fear in her eyes.

"Yeah, I think so."

Evan was panting as if he had just run a marathon. His baseball cap was no longer on his head, nor were his sunglasses. His right knee was sore and he was missing his right shoe. Without saying a word to each other they realized if Anna had turned in the other direction, the car would have slid down the steep mountainside into the ocean. They sighed heavily with relief.

"What happened?" Anna asked.

"You almost killed us trying to avoid a deer."

"That's right, Evan! Just blame me," she cried.

"I don't want to fight, Anna."

She apologized and asked him whether he was okay.

"Yeah, just a little shook up, that's all," he said.

They were stuck at the bottom of the incline and needed help in pulling the car back onto the road. They called for a tow truck and in a few hours they were soon on their way to the resort. The accident put them both in a somber mood as they understood they could have easily lost their lives. Anna drove slowly and quietly to the resort at Bodega Bay.

They were up early the next morning. Anna drank a cup of coffee as she pondered whether she did the right thing by coming to Bodega Bay. She was beginning to think their brush with death was some kind of omen that maybe it was not a good idea after all. Evan sat quietly on the small sofa drinking a cup of tea. He looked pensive and uncomfortable as he watched Anna unpack their bags.

They would be there for a couple of days and she soon had everything organized and put away. They both sat quietly without a word. The only sound was the roar of the ocean from the open window. It was one of those days a burning fire could be very romantic for a young couple in love. The silence was broken by Evan. He wanted to know why they were there and was it really necessary to go so far to talk. Anna remained silent as she gathered her thoughts. She promised herself she would not allow anger and frustration to overtake her desire to find answers.

"Evan, I think it's obvious that in spite of the fact that I love you, our relationship is incomplete. I have spent many nights trying to examine whether I have failed as a wife after only one year of marriage. I have questioned whether I have done something that has turned you off from me as a woman. I have not come up with any answers other than you appear not to want me. You seem to have no interest in consummating our marriage like most normal couples do. You tell me you love me, but in that way you are a stranger. I have done everything I can think of to express my deep love for you and fought with myself over what I'm doing wrong. I have finally decided that it's now up to you to explain what's happening on your end and what we can do to change things and make our marriage work on all levels, especially when it comes to our lack of intimacy."

Evan was quiet and Anna could see he was uncomfortable. He looked like a trapped animal as he began searching for a way to escape. He finally spoke up. "I can only tell you that I love you, Anna, and you have to believe me. There are things I cannot share with you, even though you are my wife."

"Like what?" she demanded, her voice rising in anger. "I'm your wife and I should know everything about you, Evan. We are married, don't you understand that?"

"Yes, I understand. I'm not a goddamn fool and I wish you would stop talking about this topic."

"Stop talking, are you crazy? We are married and you have never touched me like a husband is supposed to touch his wife."

"I'm busy with other things, Anna. I have my law school studies and everything else, don't you know that?"

"I only know that I married a man who is either dishonest or does not love me."

"I do love you, sweetheart, I swear."

"Bullshit!! You have a fucked up way of showing your love, buddy! What's wrong with you, Evan? Are you gay or something?"

"No, you know that's silly."

"Then what is the problem?"

He suddenly looked at her from across the room with tears in his eyes. He bowed his head, eyes riveted to the floor, shoulders hunched. He looked like a small boy who had done something wrong and was afraid to tell his mother what it was. Her anger and frustration subsided as she felt sorrow for her husband. She saw a man with something he would never share with her. For the first time, she had an overwhelming feeling that whatever his problem was, it was bigger than their marriage. Anna left the room and Evan remained sitting on the sofa, staring out the window on a cool gray day in Bodega Bay.

They returned from Bodega Bay and the next few weeks Anna threw herself into her job. She was now a Vice President and it required an immense amount of time and effort to be successful in her new position. In a way she was happy about that, because she did not have too much time to think about her relationship with Evan. He was still working at Bloomingdales and preparing for his last year of law school. He was planning to take the bar next year. They both would get home late in the evening. Evan was usually studying until he fell asleep in the den. Anna would spend hours on the computer at night preparing for work the next day. All of their time and energy was spent working or studying.

They were like two ghosts, passing in the night but not really communicating unless it was absolutely necessary. The relationship seemed worse since the trip to Bodega Bay and there was no real resolution. She had a strong feeling that Evan was fast losing interest in her or in staying in the same house. When they happened to bump into each other in the house, he avoided eye contact and many times would duck into another room to avoid her. He would spend much of his time in the law library until late at night. Sometimes they would go for three or four days without seeing each other.

She was at work most of the day and he would leave his job and go directly to study at night. It seemed ridiculous that two people in the same house could have divorced themselves mentally and physically from each other. What really hurt Anna was that as miserable as she was, Evan seemed to be fine. She could overhear him laughing with his friends on the phone talking about one thing or another. But it hurt to hear him laughing and joking and seeming happy when talking to others, but not her. She was beginning to think that Evan did not love her and she was a complete failure as a wife. She was afraid and lonely.

Simone Sason had only spent a few minutes socializing with Anna at the wedding. She was introduced to her by Frederic, Evan's father. She thought Anna seemed like such a wholesome young American, just like the kind you see in the movies. She was intelligent, optimistic and naive. But she could tell there was something special about Anna. She had a sense of decency that appealed to Simone, and she wanted to get to know her. She would be traveling to San Francisco in a month and wanted to see Anna while she was there. There were things Anna should know, but Simone had not decided whether she would share them with Anna. Anna received a telephone call at her office late Friday afternoon.

"Hello, Anna speaking."

"Hello, Anna, it's Simone."

"Who?"

"Simone Sason, your father-in-law's associate from Athens. I met you last year at your beautiful wedding in Carmel."

"Oh, yeah, Simone, I do remember you."

Anna was curious why this woman she had only met once would call her. Anna did not care for Frederic and anybody associated with him was not necessarily someone she wanted to know or spend time with.

"Anna, I know that you don't know me well, but if you would share a little of your time with me, I would like to talk with you."

Anna was busy and not necessarily interested in spending time with this woman.

"Evan is very busy and I don't know if we will have time to spend time with anyone. He is studying hard in law school."

"Oh no, Anna, I only want to see you, dear."

Anna's curiosity overrode her lack of interest in meeting Simone. She agreed to meet her at the Slanted Door restaurant. Anna had a taste for Asian food, and she loved the bourbon they served.

Anna entered the restaurant and Simone was already seated at the table. She looked glamorous as usual. She wore a black and white Givenchy suit, leopard spotted shoes, and a small black veil with a small white hat. She stood out among the other diners and got more than a few glances from some of the men in the place. She looked like one of those Euro party people you see in the movies and magazines. When she spotted Anna a big smile spread across her face as she rose from the table and gave Anna the two-cheek Euro kiss. Anna gave her a hesitant hug. The type you give people you would really prefer not to hug. Anna sat and ordered a bourbon and Simone followed her lead by having the same thing.

"Thank you for meeting with me, Anna. You look great and your wedding was one of the most beautiful ceremonies I have ever attended."

"Thank you, everyone seemed to enjoy themselves that day."

"It's good to be in San Francisco. I see you choose a beautiful restaurant, where I hear the food is excellent."

"Yeah, I eat here often and it's very popular in the city."

"How is your husband, Anna?'

"He's fine."

"I know you don't know me well, Anna, so I will tell you a little about my background. I was born in Romania but moved as a child to Greece. In college, I studied business at the National University of Athens. When I completed college, I began a consulting business and sold off the business after a few years to focus on managing mergers between various companies."

During dinner, Anna became a little more relaxed with Simone. She found her funny and very interesting. Simone was married twice before, both times to the wrong man, she would quickly add with a sly smile. She was no doubt a self-made woman of the world. Anna could not help but wonder about Simone's relationship with Frederic. Were they having an affair? And where was his wife during the wedding last year? They had a few more drinks and began to really talk.

"Simone, we have only met once and you seemed like a decent person, but what do you want from me?"

"I only seek your friendship, Anna. I have worked with your father-in-law Frederic for a number of years and I have learned a lot as his principal partner in business. We have become very close over the years. Some say we are too close, since he does have a wife, and I am a single woman. I find those comments comical since my close friends know I'm a lesbian and he's not my type, if you know what I mean," she laughed. "I can only tell you that he is a man that you can respect and admire for his accomplishments but not one to trust. I saw the look in your eyes the day of the wedding when you greeted Frederic. I knew then you did not like him. I also knew it was understandable, because I know how he can be with those he views as a threat. Frederic is a very wealthy man worth hundreds of millions of dollars, and Evan is his only heir. In the past he made it clear that Evan should never get married because it would be a threat to the family's fortune. He believed there are many women who would seek Evan out for his money and it was his job to protect him from those types of people. I'm sure that is one of the reasons he did not like you or was not particularly pleased Evan married you."

It was a revelation but not a total surprise, Anna thought. "If protecting Evan from women who were out to gain access to his wealth was one of the reasons for his father's attitude, what were the other reasons?" she asked.

Simone stared down at the table as if she suddenly found the silverware fascinating.

"There are things I cannot share with you Anna, but I will when the time is right." Anna was very curious but decided not to ask any more questions. She sensed it would not be wise to question her further. Simone changed the topic.

"Anna, you have been married over a year, are you happy?" Anna wondered why she would ask her about her marriage unless she knew something Anna didn't. Anna became uncomfortable and began looking for a reason to leave. But she also felt Simone's intentions were good and she wanted to support Anna. She opened up to Simone and told her she was not happy. Maybe it was the bourbon, or just a desperate need to tell someone who was not a family member or a friend. She felt that others would see her as a failed wife if they knew the truth about the crux of her marital problems.

Simone reached across the table without saying a word and held Anna's hand the way one would a child's hand. She gently rubbed her hand and smiled the way a mother would. For some reason, Anna felt comforted.

She then said something strange. "A time will come when you will need answers for a challenge you will face in the future. When that time comes, I will help, do you understand?" Anna said yes, although she was not sure what Simone meant. Before leaving the restaurant, Simone leaned over and whispered into Anna's ear, "Your husband's fate has already been decided." She turned and walked out of the restaurant, raising her umbrella high above her head as she disappeared into the pouring rain. Anna was confused about what had just happened in the last two hours. She decided she would not share her conversation with Simone with anyone, even Evan.

Over the next few days she tried to put her meeting with Simone in context by asking herself questions. *Why did she seek me out? Does she know something important that I don't? What is her real relationship with Frederic? Did Frederic send her here to learn something about me and Evan?* She had no real answers, but she had a strong feeling that she would be in touch with Simone in the future. One thing she wanted to understand was how Frederic's wealth would impact her and Evan. Should she be concerned, and more importantly, what were Evan's thoughts on this?

Anna and Evan never talked a lot about money. Anna knew Evan's father was rich, but never connected it to Evan other than that his father paid his law school expenses. She did not know he was an heir until she was told by Simone. She did not really care for Frederic, so she never brought his name up in conversations with Evan unless it was absolutely necessary. It seemed each time they would discuss him, it was negative.

He would still call Evan late at night from Europe and get into loud arguments over things she had no knowledge of. Evan would usually end up screaming at his father like a maniac and slamming down the phone in anger. Anna figured Frederic did not approve of her because he thought she was some type of gold-digger. This hurt Anna, because if Frederic had made an effort to know her just a little, he would have known better. But he seemed to be wrapped up in his wealth and his business brilliance without the desire or capacity to see people for who they really were. She was now curious to know about the circumstances surrounding Evan's wealth and what it would mean for their future.

She wanted to talk with Evan, but they had not held a real conversation since returning from Bodega Bay. She decided to change the mood at home by surprising him. She cooked a special dinner capped off with a bottle of his favorite Chianti from the Napa Valley. Anna texted him during the day asking him to come home early because she had a surprise. He walked into the house and broke into a big smile and beamed with delight when he saw the dinner she had prepared.

"WOW! What a surprise. Did you get another promotion at work?"

"No, I decided it was time that we have a decent meal for a change and act a little more civilized with each other."

He looked at her curiously without speaking. He did not want to get into an argument, so he kept his mouth shut and prepared to eat dinner and enjoy a bottle of Ruffino Ducale Oro. They talked for a few hours over dinner and candlelight. The wine had put them in a mellow mood. They desperately missed each other although they live under the same roof. Anna felt the mood was right to question Evan about his father's wealth and Frederic's plans for Evan.

"Evan, you never told me much about your father's wealth."

"Where did that topic come from?"

"We have never discussed it, so maybe it's time we do. I'm sure at some point it will have an impact if we stay married." Anna said.

"Stay married! Are you planning to divorce me anytime soon?" he asked.

"No, but I think this is something we need to talk about."

"Yeah, you're right, I have been thinking about it also. What do you want to know?"

"What is the financial relationship between you and your father?"

"I'm the sole heir to the estate if my father dies. My father is worth approximately 400 million dollars in investments and other stuff."

"400 million dollars! Holy shit! I cannot believe it. I knew he was rich, but that is crazy."

Evan laughed at her reaction. "When I turn 30 years old I will inherit a portion that is worth about 100 million dollars." "

"What! I cannot believe it. Why haven't you told me all of this?"

"I don't know; I didn't think it was that important. I was going to wait until I turned 30 next year and tell you then."

Anna was shocked. She had no idea Evan's wealth would be that great. *Simone may have been right. Frederic is concerned that I will have access to Evan's money and eventually his estate, and he does not want that,* she thought

CHAPTER

5

Madison was concerned about Anna and her marital problems. But Anna was now a married woman and it was not Madison's place to interfere in matters between Anna and Evan. She decided not to do or say anything unless Anna asked for help. Her attitude changed when she ran into an old high school friend at Whole Foods.

Madison was standing in line when she felt someone tap her on the shoulder from behind. She turned and a tall guy with an athletic build and the whitest teeth she had ever seen gave her a big bear hug. "Madison, it's me, Danny Zazo from Seacliff High School, you silly skank," he laughed. She looked closer and soon recognized him. She was shocked at how different he looked since high school. Back in the day, Danny was a classic dork. He had bad hair, bad clothes and bad breath.

She could not believe how much he had changed. He looked like a Greek God. He had grown to six feet, his body ripped with a small waist and big biceps. He wore a short tapered haircut like the guy's in San Francisco. His overall handsomeness was shocking to behold. She could not help but think about a film she saw once where an ugly hairy caterpillar was transformed into a beautiful butterfly. Danny was now a butterfly.

"I cannot believe it's you. You look fantastic, Danny."

"Yeah, well, it's been ten years and people change, ya know?"

"What are you up to these days, Danny?"

"I own a string of health clubs in Malibu, La Jolla and a few in Santa Monica."

While Danny updated Madison on the past ten years she could not help but think that he had some type of plastic surgery. *He did not look this damn good in high school, she thought.* She knew people changed over the years, but not this much.

After a few minutes of polite conversation, Madison gave him a goodbye hug and told him it was great to see him again. She was about to get into her car when she heard someone yelling out her name across the parking lot. She looked and Danny was jogging over towards her with that same silly grin he'd had in high school.

"Hey, I forgot to ask you about your old friend Anna Cain. Do you ever hear from her?"

"Yeah, we still talk, she's living in the

East Bay."

"Did you know I had a mad crush on her in high school?"

"Really? I didn't know that."

"I was wondering whether you could give her my contact info, just in case she might want to get together to have a cup of coffee or something. You know what I mean?"

"Yeah, I do. Take care, Danny, it was good seeing you again."

"Oh, by the way, if you guys are ever in L.A., you have a place to stay. I have a beach house in Laguna and you're welcome anytime. Take care, Madison, hope to hear from you soon."

"Bye, Danny."

Madison stood in the middle of the parking lot in momentary shock. Who would have thought dorky Danny Zazo still had a crush on Anna, ten years after high school? Madison's mind started to work at a rapid pace. She laughed when she thought of the possibilities with Danny Zazo and Anna. Under normal circumstances she would have mentioned to him that Anna was happily married and not to waste his time. But she said nothing and was not sure why. Should she tell Anna? *Would this be a partial answer to Anna's problem if she hooked up with Danny?* she wondered. Madison was the Maid of Honor at Anna's wedding and now she was having devilish thoughts about Anna and Danny. A slight smile appeared on her face the more she thought about it. *Anna deserves some happiness*, she thought.

Anna was upset and frustrated with the way things were going between her and Evan. Her only solution was to throw herself into her work one hundred percent. She would leave home at 6:00 AM and return in the evening after 9:00 PM, sometimes later. She only thought about work. She did her best not to allow her relationship with Evan to invade her thoughts, but she was not always successful. She felt she needed a change, but did not know what kind of change or how to go about it.

The next morning her boss called her into the office for a chat. She had no idea what he wanted except he had a goofy smile on his face. "Anna, I wanted to thank you personally for the job you did on Amtex. That deal will add 10% to our profit margin, and that's good news. I know you are on the fast track in the company and I'm willing to do everything I can to help you move forward." Anna remained quiet and listened.

She knew from the way he was kissing her ass he had something else in mind. "We will be opening the new Omega series in Los Angeles next month. I need someone of your caliber to spend at least a few months down there to get things off with a bang. It will mean a big bonus and a lot of face time with the CEO. When they asked who I was thinking about sending down to Los Angeles, I mentioned you and they were pleased. What do you think?"

"I don't know Phil, I have responsibilities here at home with Evan and other things."

"You should think about what this could mean for your career, Anna." She told him she would think it over and left for home. This was a big opportunity and she would be the first woman to hold such a position. She was excited, but torn about what to do. This could also be the change she had been looking for. It would mean leaving Evan at home, but maybe it would be good that they would be separated for a while. He could come to L.A. for weekends and she could return home to the Bay Area on certain weekends.

When she told Evan, he did not seem to be that concerned about her leaving home for a few months. His enthusiasm was notably muted. He basically said have fun and to let him know when he could visit her. He never mentioned that he would miss her and how it would impact them being away from each other for the first time since getting married. He seemed almost cavalier about her leaving. His attitude helped her to make the decision to take on the new assignment in L.A. She was angry he did not seem to care that she would no longer be home each night for a few months. The next day she called her boss and told him she was excited about the new assignment and ready to go to work. A week later, she left for L.A.

Evan sat on the sofa in the dark with a beer in his hand, staring at the living room wall. The house was cold and quiet. Anna had been in L.A. for three weeks and he was starting to feel alone. He was wondering how to handle their relationship. He wanted to ask his father for advice, but he knew what Frederic would say. He would tell Evan to divorce Anna for her own good. He could hear his father's voice as he imagined what he would say if he was there with Evan. *"You were never meant to be like everyone else. I have told you a thousand times. Your fate in this world is clear, and you had better understand that before it's too late."*

Evan became emotional as he thought about the complications in his life. He loved Anna with all his heart, but she would never understand who or what he was. He knew over the past year he'd acted like a real asshole at times. He thought Anna might become tired of his antics and divorce him. In the long run, that might be good for both of them. He wondered whether he should have followed his father's advice and not gotten married. He thought long and hard about it, but his love for Anna was so powerful he had to be with her, even if it wasn't for very long.

Anna received a text from Madison, she was in LA. She asked Anna to meet her for dinner later that evening. Anna was hesitant because she had to be at work early the next day and had to prepare for an important presentation. But it was hard to turn down her best friend. They met at Spangles in West Hollywood. Anna was tired and hungry, but she was looking forward to seeing Madison. For the past three weeks she'd worked ten hour days, ate takeout and stayed up late working on her laptop.

She arrived at the restaurant at 7:00 P.M. It was filled with glam people with multicolored hair, body-revealing clothes, metal piercings extending from ears, tongues and who knows where else. There were actors, musicians, and wannabes. Anna laughed and thought of it like taking a trip to Disneyland. You see all types, but it was strictly Fantasyland and not to be taken seriously.

She looked around just as Madison walked through the door of the restaurant. You could not miss her with her rainbow colored hair, five-inch banana yellow high heel shoes, both ears with at least eight or nine ear rings in each ear and a dress that Anna could only consider otherworldly. "Hey, girlfriend, what's up?" she yelled across the restaurant.

"Hey, Maddie, how ya doing?"

"I'm cool, I'm so happy you made it."

They gave each other a long, warm hug. It was good seeing Madison again, but Anna could not stop staring at her and finally asked, "What in the hell are you wearing?" She was trying to muffle her laugh. She looked like a float in the Rose Bowl parade with the different colors she was wearing and the huge multicolored dreadlocks that covered her head. *Bob Marley would be proud*, she thought. Madison laughed at Anna's question. She said she was in L.A. on business. She and some guy were beginning a website that sold baby clothes and they were meeting in LA with potential buyers. Anna felt much better when she saw Madison and a few drinks later they were screaming with laughter as they recalled old times.

Anna went to the ladies' room while Madison ordered more drinks. When she returned, there were two guys sitting at her table with Madison. She did not recognize either one of them. Madison blurted out, "Hey, Anna, look what the dog dragged in!" All three of them were laughing raucously as if they were all in on some joke that Anna wasn't. "Anna don't you recognize your old high school mate Danny Zazo?" Madison asked.

"Who?"

"Hey, Anna, it's me, Danny the dork, remember?"

She took a few seconds and stared at the guy with the big smile, deep tan and very white teeth. Her mind reeled as she tried to remember him. While he continued talking, she did start to remember. "Oh yeah, Danny, I remember you."

"It's nice to see you Anna, you look great."

"You look totally different, Danny."

"Thanks, Anna. You know, I'm considered hot property here in L.A."

"What do you mean?"

"I own 15 elite health clubs in the most exclusive locations in L.A. and I am considered one of the most eligible bachelors in the city."

"Yeah! can you believe how great this guy looks, Anna?" asked Madison. "I have a new name for him."

"What is it?" Anna asked.

"I now call him Danny Butterfly because of the way this hot hunk changed himself since high school. He went from King of the Dorks to this, can you believe it?"

All three of them thought it was funny, but Anna didn't. She remembered why she could not remember this guy, because she had tried so hard to forget him in high school. He was not a bad guy, just someone she had absolutely no interest in but he never did seem to understand that. He did look great with the buffed body, white teeth, and obviously some work done on his face and ears. Anna did not remember his ears being that small in high school. He'd had big ears and all the kids used to call him Dumbo behind his back after the cute elephant in the Disney cartoons with the large, floppy ears.

When Anna made it clear that she was married, the atmosphere at the table became subdued. She was pissed off at Madison for not telling Danny in the first place and she had no interest in hooking up with Danny Butterfly, or whatever Maddie was calling him. The mood shifted and for some reason Danny suddenly found Madison fascinating, and they got into an intense conversation about who knows what. After a while Danny finally introduced his friend Mark, who had been sitting not saying much except when he would laugh at some silly comment Danny or Madison made. He was a psychiatrist, and one of Danny's close friends. He was also an investor in Danny's company.

Mark had one of those cool bald heads that only certain guys could wear and look good. Michael Jordan was the only guy that Anna thought looked good with that style, but this guy looked cool also. He had a look of sophistication and wisdom about him that Anna could not quite place. She could tell he was older but when he laughed, there was a youthful energy about him she found appealing. He was very tan with a nice physique and seemed at ease with himself. She caught him sneaking glances at her across the table and she was curious about him, but would never admit it to anyone including herself.

Mark and Anna tried to have a cordial conversation by default, since there was no one else to talk with at the same table. The music in the restaurant had become very loud and the crowd had grown much larger. They decided to leave the table and go out onto the patio where they could actually hear what the other was saying. Madison and Danny never realized they had left for the patio. They were heavily engrossed and looking into each other's eyes.

Danny realized after ten years he had no chance with Anna, so he decided to hit on Madison. Madison seemed to be really impressed with Danny. Maybe it was the plastic surgery and the health clubs he owned. Anna giggled to herself the more she thought about it.

Anna and Mark stood on the patio balcony overlooking the Hollywood Hills. They could finally talk and hear each other as they laughed about how loud it was inside and how Madison and Danny never missed them when they left the table. Anna told him what she did for a living and that she was happily married. He smiled and said, "Marriage is a mixture of two elements, divine love and passion, the strongest bond there is between a man and a woman."

Anna was taken back by his statement. She had never heard it put quite that way and thought it was profound. He also surprised her by telling her he went to the same high school she had ten years earlier. They both laughed when she told him that some of the same boring teachers were still there when she graduated years later. They both had a good laugh as they called off the names of their old teachers.

Mark became friends with Danny when they met casually at one of the health clubs and struck up a friendship, then discovered they were alumni of the same high school. He was from Tiburon and his family ran a boat shop on the Sausalito pier. He said he was born in the water and had webbed feet. Anna laughed and thought the good doctor was funny, even though he was a shrink. He had a very successful practice in L.A. and was well known in Hollywood as one of the guys the stars would seek out for help when needed.

"Are you famous?" Anna asked.

"No, I'm not, the people I treat are famous, and that's the way I like to keep it," he laughed.

They soon realized they had been talking for over two hours and enjoying every minute of it. Anna had never met such an intelligent, intuitive man.

He had travelled widely and seen many things and had many experiences in his 38 years. There was something almost feminine about his energy. He spoke with an ease that made her relax. She never felt that nervous tension that women sometime feel in the company of strange men. Sometimes when you meet a man for the first time, they will try to hit on you, whether you're married or not, especially in L.A. She did not feel that with Mark. During their conversation he asked whether she was experiencing serious stress in her life.

"Oh no, Mark, please don't play shrink with me," she laughed.

"Anna, please do not take my words the wrong way, but with some people I can hear certain stresses in their voices that usually indicate an underlying problem, that's all I meant. I'm sorry if I offended you."

"No, I'm just surprise you can tell something like that by just talking to someone."

"Usually I can't, unless the person is experiencing something deep and troubling in their life and it becomes apparent after a while."

Anna swallowed hard and felt it was time to go home. She had a long day at work the next day and it was already past her bedtime. Madison and Danny had disappeared and Mark walked her to the car. "I enjoyed meeting you, Anna. Here is my contact information and please don't hesitate to call me about anything, do you understand?" For some reason she said yes, and felt good after she said it. Before going to bed, she checked her phone messages and had a garbled message from Madison. It was something about being at Danny's beach house in Laguna and she could see the stars. Anna laughed and went to bed.

During the next few weeks Mark remained on Anna's mind. She had never met anyone like him and was wondering if she should call him to say hello. Her curiosity was not based upon his attractiveness; after all, she was married and loyal to Evan. But she could not shake the feeling she got when she was with him that evening on the restaurant patio. The feeling of calm she experienced listening to him talk. She figured because he was a psychiatrist, he knew how to make people feel relaxed and secure within themselves. She was not quite sure why, but she felt compelled to at least speak with him again, soon.

Anna had been working long hours over the past six weeks and finally had a free weekend. She called Evan right after work Friday night. She was excited about seeing him the next day. But he surprised her by going camping with some of his law school buddies rather than spending the weekend with her.

Initially they agreed they would try and see each other every weekend. She would fly up to the Bay Area or he would fly down to L.A. Because of her work commitments and what appeared to be Evan's busy schedule, they only seen each other once in the past three months. They communicated by text or a periodic phone call.

Anna could not put her finger on it, but something was different about Evan. He seemed distant and quiet the few times they saw each other. She felt the connection between them had become weaker. She went days without thinking about Evan, which was unusual. In the past, he was never really far from her mind. She was not sure why, maybe because of the way he treated her and his odd behavior, or just her frustration with the way things were between them.

She was not going to allow her free weekend to be spent worrying about Evan. She decided to lay out by the hotel pool and get some sun. She grabbed a beach towel and laid out by the pool for several hours, capped off by a shot of bourbon. She examined her body in her old swimsuit and was not happy with what she saw. She was ten pounds' overweight after months of working long hours and gorging herself with food after getting home from work late each night. She knew she needed to begin an exercise program, lose weight and get into shape. That afternoon she received a text from

Madison inviting her to one of the health clubs owned by Danny. Anna could not believe the timing of Madison's invite; it was perfect. She agreed to meet Madison in Santa Monica at the health club.

The New Centurion Health Club in Santa Monica was very nice and very L.A. *People literally worship their bodies down here,* she thought. Celebrities were known to frequent the place and there was every type of amenity imaginable. Madison met Anna in the lobby of the spacious facility. Madison was dressed totally in purple. Her leotards, sneakers, scarf, headband, gym bag, etc. She looked like a large grape with legs.

Anna could not stop giggling when she saw Madison. "I know you are laughing at my outfit, Anna, you skank," Madison laughed. "You know I have to be me." She gave Anna a warm hug and was happy to see her friend.

Anna was curious and asked Madison, "How did you get access to this place? I understand it's private and admission is difficult for non-members. Is that true?"

"Yeah, but I have this special card." She pulled out a gold card with the letters VIP printed on the card rather than her name. Danny had this special card made for her to gain entrance anytime she desired.

"My God, Maddie! Are you and Danny going together, or what?"

"Let's just say he and I are very close," she smiled.

"What happened to the French guy you were dating?"

"Oh yeah, I had to dump him a month ago. He never told me he had a wife in Paris and two small kids. The woman with the kids was his third wife in the last seven years. He was a lying French asshole," she laughed.

Anna was dumbfounded and joined Madison in laughing at such a crazy situation.

Madison escorted Anna around the facility as if she was a celebrity. Other club members would stare as Madison explained all the activities the club offered. This was not normally done, except for celebrities.

When members saw Anna being escorted by Madison they assumed she was somebody famous, so heads turned as she and Madison strolled through the club. Everyone knew that Madison was connected to Danny and he owned the club. If Anna was with Madison, then she must be important. Anna could not keep a straight face as Madison continued her tour and people just gawked at Anna and tried to figure out which celebrity she was. She was having fun and spent the next half hour laughing with Madison about one silly thing or another.

"Are you ready for your first work out, Anna?" Madison asked.

"Yeah, look at my hips," she laughed.

"Well, you could afford to lose a few pounds, but don't worry, I've got just the guy for you. He's one of the best trainers here at the club."

"Wait a minute, Madison, I haven't worked out in over a year and I am in terrible shape. I'm not ready for some buffed out trainer who will just embarrass me because I can hardly do a push up."

"Don't worry about it," she said. Madison disappeared and minutes later a tall blonde young guy, about 22, walked up to Anna with his hand outstretched. "Hi, I'm Brock Branford, and I will be your trainer today."

She looked at him and smiled. She thought, *My God, this is all I need, some guy who looks like a Viking who will no doubt cause me pain and anguish before this is over*. He had a broad, tan face, big dimples, and a great body. She was sure he was one of those guys who spent all his spare time looking in the mirror as he worked out 24/7. She finally spoke up as Brock just stood there and smiled at her. "Hi, I'm Anna. It's nice to meet you, Brock." He put her through a workout routine that made her have second thoughts about coming back to the gym, but two hours later she was sore but felt wonderful. After the stretching, lifting and pulling she felt invigorated and decided she was going to start a workout routine and attend the club regularly.

Anna was starting to miss home, but she was also enjoying L.A. She had a great job and was excelling at her new assignment. She was at the gym two or three times a week and her energy level was super. It was a good move because her job was demanding and staying in shape physically was a necessity. Sometimes during a quiet moment, she would think about Evan. He seldom called anymore, and it was almost like they were two old friends who had sort of moved on with their lives. That really scared her because she was not at the point in their relationship where a permanent separation was a possibility. Sometimes after a fight with him she would think about it, but nothing more than that.

It was L.A.'s worst storm in years. Anna had completed her workout and was on her way back to her hotel when it was announced on the radio that traffic was congested and the freeway was closed. The roads were flooded and there was no way to reach her hotel. She was not sure what to do, so she called Madison. Madison told her she would take care of it. She told Anna to head back to the gym and she would meet her there. Anna was able to get back to the gym by sheer luck and help from a traffic cop. She sat in the lobby of the gym and minutes later a black Mercedes SUV drove into the parking lot. Madison jumped out of the SUV in her camouflage green rain gear and rushed into the lobby. She greeted Anna with a big warm hug.

"Hey, home girl, you ok?"

"Yeah, just a little wet," Anna laughed.

"Let's get the hell out of here," Maddie said.

They both scampered outside and got quickly into the warm dry vehicle.

"Most of the traffic problems and flooding are in the opposite direction from where we are going, so don't worry. You can stay at our place tonight and we can work something out tomorrow." "That sounds great Maddie," Anna said gratefully.

An hour later they arrived at Danny's beach house, which sat on the side of a hill away from the street and the waist high rainwater. Danny

was happy to see Anna and glad she was safe.
The house was beautiful, with tall ceilings,
huge fireplaces, glass walls, etc. It was a
beautiful home that looked like something out
of a Frank Lloyd Wright exposé on modern
architecture. Anna dried off and had a glass of
wine with Madison and Danny while his house
chef cooked dinner. Danny was living large and
he and Madison seemed happy as they sat close
together on a large, green velvet sofa. Danny
said he would like to meet Evan sometime so
he could meet the lucky guy who hooked Anna.
They both laughed, but Anna could sense that
he still had a little thing for her in spite of
Madison sitting next to him. They were about
to have dinner when the doorbell rang. Danny
opened the door and proclaimed loudly for all
to hear, "Hey! My main man is here!" Anna and
Madison looked over and standing in the foyer
was Mark in yellow rain gear with a big smile
on his face.

"Hey everyone, the rain man is here," he
laughed. It was a stupid joke, but everyone
laughed, including Anna. Maybe she laughed

because it was Mark, maybe not; she wasn't sure.

Mark and Danny had a big meeting tomorrow with a venture capitalist group and they had to plan for the meeting. They were going to use Danny's place to do a little work after dinner. Madison gave him a nice hug and welcomed him into the house. His eyes were riveted on Anna when he saw her sitting across the room. She immediately sat up and smiled when she saw him. She had not seen or spoken to him since the night on the restaurant patio. On several occasions she'd wanted to call him, but hadn't. She did not think it was right, although she thought about him numerous times. She even had a dream about him one night and masturbated in her sleep. She was embarrassed about the entire event. It was not the type of thing a married woman did, she reasoned to herself.

Everyone had a great time over dinner. The food and company were excellent and Madison and Danny were a regular comedy show. This was the most fun Anna had had since she moved to L.A. She was really surprised how Danny and Madison seemed to gel together. She knew her friend well and she could tell there were heavy sparks between them. Danny and Mark worked in the office for a few hours after dinner. Later they joined Anna and Madison in the den to have a night cap of scotch on the rocks. The guys joined in and soon everyone was laughing and talking about movies, politics, money, and relationships. Everyone was quiet while Danny gave his opinion on relationships. "I think a good relationship is keeping your lady happy. Get her a new car every year, take her to Europe or the Caribbean, and provide her with the necessities of life like jewels and money," he laughed.

Madison blurted out, "Right on, Danny! You got the right answer." Everyone fell over laughing. Mark and Anna were in tears from laughing at Danny's comments. Danny was not sure what they were laughing at, since that was his truth when it came to relationships. It was clear those were Madison's views also.

"What do you think about relationships, Mark?" asked Danny. "You're a shrink, you must have opinions."

Anna became very attentive as they listened to Mark speak. "I want to make it clear that I'm speaking as a 38-year-old single guy, not just a psychiatrist. I think it's important to distinguish between the two. I have drawn my conclusions about love and relationships based upon observation and personal experience." Anna could feel the blood in her body simmer as her excitement increased when he began speaking. "We enter relationships full of fantasies and naiveté, like adolescents. And often, the beginning of a relationship is a wonderful time. But it is also a dream state. Sooner or later, problems arise and when they do, we naturally think that the problem lies with ourselves, with the other person, or with the relationship.

Then we may move on, or become depressed and give up on the possibility of love. Or perhaps even worse, we remain in the relationship, even for years as the love dies and the energy goes flat or turns nasty. We may not realize that love takes deep work and awareness of ourselves. It takes an awareness that relating deeply with another person will bring up deep, unconscious issues. We are not born knowing how to love. We are born knowing how to have sex and how to be spontaneous and alive. But turning aliveness and attraction into love is a totally different story."

When he finished, the room was quiet. The others stared at Mark and did not utter a word. Anna sat transfixed. It was the first time in her life that someone had so clearly explained the complexity of relationships between men and women, and much of what he said was uncomfortably close to her relationship with Evan. She was stunned. "Why are you guys so quiet?" Mark asked. "Did I say something wrong? are my views too New Age for you?" he laughed.

"No! God, no, it was one of the most profound things I have ever heard in my life," Anna said. When she spoke her eyes were moist and the sincerity in her voice was unmistakable. Even Madison and Danny spoke up.

"Wow! That was pretty heavy, Mark. I guess that's why you're a shrink," said Danny.

"I've developed my views from living and learning from others. Some of it has come from my practice, but the majority comes from being curious about people,"Mark said.

Danny persuaded Mark to spend the night since it was late and the storm was still raging. Later in the evening he and Madison decided to turn in for the night. Anna had her own bedroom upstairs, and Mark had another room near the patio on the ocean side of the house. Danny's stereo pumped music throughout the house with speakers everywhere. He taught Mark how to operate it and Mark played some of his and Anna's favorite music while they talked about everything under the sun. They enjoyed each other's company and the wine they drank earlier didn't hurt the flow of conversation. In spite of the wind and rain outside, the mood in the vast room was warm and mellow.

They sat in silence listening to jazz musician Toots Thielemans. They stared out the large plate glass window into the pitch black outside. There was something oddly romantic about being so close to the ocean but not able to see it because of the darkness. There was an ethereal quality to the setting as the roar of the powerful waves splashed onto the beach near midnight.

The storm became worse as huge raindrops pummeled the window like bullets and water raced down the glass panes like giant tears as they stared and listen to the tune 'Blusette.' Anna could tell that Mark knew she wanted to remain quiet. He did not say anything or move; he simply sat and stared out the window. That's one of the things she liked about him. She did not have to say anything about not wanting to talk or be alone; he knew. But he could also tell she wanted him to stay with her in the room.

After a while he decided to leave Anna alone. He said good night and headed to his room. He gave Anna a hug and told her this was one of the best evenings he'd had in a long time. She felt the same way. Before he let her go, he gave a her a quick kiss. He quickly pulled back and smiled. She did not know what to do. The quick kiss was electric, and it roared throughout her body. She wanted him to continue kissing her, but she could never do that. After all, she was a married woman, she told herself. When he left, she was dizzy with a range of feelings. She felt guilty, passionate, foolish, loving, and more. She had a last glass of wine and went to bed. She knew this guy had a strong effect on her and she knew exactly why, and that scared her.

It was 1:20 in the morning and Anna could not sleep. For the past two hours she'd only thought about Mark. She had only met the guy twice and did not know much about him, but the effect he was having on her was unbelievable. *I must forget about this and go to sleep*, she thought. Before she dozed off to sleep, she got up and walked quietly down the hallway to the bathroom next to Mark's room. Leaving the bathroom, she was startled to see someone standing in the dimly lit hallway; it was Mark. "Hey, why are you up this time of night?" she asked.

"Because I could not stop thinking about you, Anna." He came closer and kissed her with an intensity she had never felt before. Before she could figure out how to respond, she was caressing him and holding on to him for dear life. They moved into his room and onto the bed.

Anna's body was screaming with 28 years of suppressed passion and desire. She had never been held that way before. The way he touched her and kissed her was beyond words. His body had a feeling to it that she could not describe. She was thrilled this highly intelligent, intuitive man wanted her as desperately as she wanted him. He introduced her to her full womanhood that night, and she cried tears of joy. The word bliss is often overused, but she now felt she understood the true meaning of the word.

Anna saw Mark a few more times, but she was having a hard time with her guilt. Even though she enjoyed her time with Mark and was fascinated by him, she still loved Evan and was still his wife. She often thought, *why couldn't I meet Mark before Evan?* The reality was she was still married to Evan. She would be leaving L.A. in a few days for home and it would be difficult to continue seeing Mark. They met for coffee a few days later, and Mark understood her situation. He asked her to call him periodically to stay in touch, and she promised she would.

Evan knew something had to change if he wanted to remain married to Anna. He knew as a man what he had to do and what was expected of him as a husband. He loved Anna more than anyone could possibly imagine. There were reasons for his behavior, but he now was going to do his best to make his wife happy, regardless of the consequences.

Anna was happy about returning home to the Bay Area. She called Evan and gave him her flight information and told him she was excited about seeing him. She told him she missed him and loved him. She was hoping for a similar response from Evan, but he remained quiet and

said he would see her at the airport. She
wanted to make a new start with Evan and was
hopeful things would work out between them.
The plane landed at San Francisco
International Airport on a rainy night. Her
heart started to race in anticipation of seeing
her husband, in spite of the problems they'd
had in the past. She wanted to make her
marriage work.

A half hour passed and Anna was beginning
to worry. Evan was not at the airport. She
called his cell and got his voicemail. She was
about to panic when she heard her name being
called by a voice she did not initially recognize.
She looked to her left and dressed in a long
blue topcoat was Miss Hattie, her next door
neighbor. "Hi, Anna, Evan asked me to give you
a ride home." Anna was shocked and angry that
Evan asked this little old lady who was partially
blind in one eye to pick her up from the airport
because he was busy. Miss Hattie had to be in
her late eighties and drove a 1957 Chevrolet
she'd bought that year.

She was a petite gray-haired lady with very thick eyeglasses. She told Anna not to worry about her driving because see could see really well as long as everything she wanted to see was on her left side. Anna smiled and gave her a nice warm hug. "Thanks for coming to pick me up, Miss Hattie." She crossed her fingers and said a silent prayer as she got into the well-kept Chevy and headed for home. She was steaming mad and wondered what in the hell kept Evan from picking her up at the airport.

Anna arrived home safely thanks to Miss Hattie. Evan was not home yet and the house was a mess with a large pile of dirty dishes in the kitchen sink. Her cat, Cleo, looked like she had not eaten in several days. Anna decided to try and calm down before Evan returned home, although she was still angry with him. If he had been home when she arrived from the airport earlier, their might have been a physical altercation between them, she thought. She did not want that. Thirty minutes later, she heard Evan walk into the house. He was whistling as if he did not have a care in the world.

Before he could say hello, she verbally pounced.

"What in the hell happened to you, Evan? Why weren't you at the airport?" Anna asked angrily.

"I had an exam that I totally forgot about, sorry about that. I saw Miss Hattie yesterday, and she agreed to pick you up from the airport."

"Why didn't you text or call me?"

"My cell phone was broken for some reason, sorry about that honey."

She was not sure whether he was lying or not, but in a way it did not matter anymore. She was quickly losing faith in Evan. Something was wrong with him and she was worried. She was also concerned about her changing feelings towards him. She thought returning home to Evan would somehow reaffirm her love and their marriage. It didn't work out that way.

She was now confused about how she really felt about her husband. She was still in love with him, but she found herself thinking more about Mark. The nights they'd spent together were like nothing she ever experienced before. It wasn't just the physical but the mental and emotional security he provided her, in a strange sort of way. The sense of guilt she experienced after spending the night with Mark was now gone. She was going back to L.A. to complete some last minute details to close out her assignment. She texted Mark asking to see him while she was there, and he agreed. She still loved Evan, but Mark had unearthed a part of her she never knew existed.

It'd been several months and Anna was back home and working hard to advance her career. Evan had improved his behavior and they were committed to trying to make things work between them. He had become more attentive and worked harder to demonstrate his love for Anna. He made a commitment to become a better husband. They had a heart to heart talk and he told her he never stopped loving her and would do anything for her. She felt guilty about her affair with Mark as she listened closely to Evan committing to making a new and better life for them. "I'm now willing to do anything to keep us together, Anna. You are my life for now and forever more." She had never heard him talk that way before.

He kissed her with more passion than any time in the past. She thought maybe she should be away from home more often if this was the reward she could expect once she returned. Anna was feeling guilty about her affair with Mark and felt she should tell Evan everything since they had both committed to being honest with each other and were trying hard to make their marriage work. She told Evan everything about Mark, including the times she'd spent the night with him over the past few months. Evan sat quietly and stared out the window as she spoke. She watched him closely. He did not utter a word. It was as if he was in a trance. She wondered what he was thinking.

Evan kept his thoughts secret and worked hard to control his rage as he listened to Anna's confession about her affair with Mark. He was angry and torn inside, but hid his new hatred for Anna and pretended he would forgive her and continue their relationship. But inside, his thinking was very different. *I will never forgive her for having an affair with some asshole in Los Angeles. All the suffering I have endured that she will never know about. I will repay her for her whorish behavior and lack of respect for me. She will regret what she has done and I will give her something she will never recover from in this life.*

He turned slowly towards Anna and asked, "Do you love this guy?"

"No, I love you."

"Are you planning to see him again?"

"No."

He told her he forgave her. "From now on, I will be the husband you thought I would be and the one you deserved." He leaned over and gave her a long, passionate kiss. She was overwhelmed with emotion as he picked her up like a child in his arms and took her into the bedroom. They made love for the first time and Anna cried with relief as the man she truly loved held her in a tight embrace, their bodies bound together as one in raw passion.

Four hours later they were still going at it like rabbits. Eventually Anna's passion dissipated, and she was extremely tired. But Evan was intense in his lovemaking. He was like a machine with no signs of fatigue or loss of energy. She thought maybe he was making up for lost time, but she had to stop him. She pushed his body off of her and left the bedroom for the kitchen. She was too tired to continue and was dying from thirst. She drank a full pitcher of water and sat on a stool to rest. She was soaking wet in perspiration and almost dehydrated. She could not believe the energy Evan had and was hoping it would not be this way each time they decided to make love.

She walked slowly back to the bedroom, hoping that he had fallen asleep. He was lying in the bed like an animal waiting for its prey. He grabbed her to continue their lovemaking, but she pleaded for him to let her take a short nap to rest. It was now 1:30 AM and she needed rest. The tugging on her arm was so strong it woke her out of a sound sleep. "Wake up, Anna!" Evan was pulling on her body as he tried to unfold her legs to gain access to her like a maniac. He wanted to continue making love after she had only slept for 20 minutes. She was scared and worried, because this was abnormal. They began again and two hours later Anna was so tired she got angry and told him to stop. He told her he wanted to continue while she slept. She wanted to say no, but this was their first time making love and she relented to his request. While she slept, he made love to her for another hour.

During the next few days Evan seemed to spend all his time trying to get her into bed. It did not matter to him if it was day or night; he seemed to have become some kind of sex fiend. She did her best to avoid him at home and he finally left her alone and became very quiet. She knew something was brewing in his mind, but she had no idea what it was.

Evan believed he had his revenge. After making love to Anna, he knew with the virus his body contained he would soon die, but he received satisfaction knowing that Anna would also die. His father told him as a teenager when he made love to a woman for the first time, she would be automatically infected with his virus and die. *I have taught her the price for being unfaithful to me. She will never be unfaithful again in this life*, he thought.

Anna was putting in long hours at work and seemed to be always tired. She felt completely run down with little or no energy. It wasn't just Evan's newly discovered sexual appetite. It was something else; it felt different. She and Evan were doing well and it seemed like each day they were becoming closer as man and wife. In spite of feeling fatigue with a lack of energy, she felt she was in pretty good shape, even though she had not gone to the gym since returning from L.A. She was really peeved at having to take an annual physical, which was company policy. She scheduled her appointment late Friday before leaving for home. When the appointment was over, she picked up one of Evan's favorite pizzas and dashed home to watch a movie that they had been dying to see on HBO. They had a great evening watching movies, drinking wine, eating pizza and having wild, uninhibited sex. Finally, life was good for Anna.

The voicemail message was from her doctor and close friend Nola Darling. She asked Anna to give her a call as soon as she got the message. Anna figured that Nola was going to hit her up to buy fundraising tickets for the Delta Sigma Ball that was held each year. Nola was the president of the oldest and most prestigious Black sorority in the nation. When Nola called anyone, she usually got a return call. Anna called her back and when Nola answered, Anna jokingly told her she was broke this year and would not be contributing any money. Nola giggled slightly, but there was a seriousness in her voice when she spoke.

"I have some important news for you, Anna."

"Is it good or bad?"

"Well, that depends on you."

"What do you mean, Nola?'

"You're ten weeks pregnant."

"Holy shit! What did you say?"

"I said you are ten weeks pregnant."

Anna seemed to momentarily lose her voice.

"Anna, are you still there?" Nola asked nervously.

"Yeah, I'm still here."

Anna could not believe it. How could she be pregnant? She'd missed her period, but that was not unusual since she had never been regular for some reason. Her family doctor told her when she was a teenager that some women's bodies just responded that way. But this was different. She had not been feeling well lately, but she attributed it to working long hours and not exercising enough. She wondered, "How could I be...?" Then it hit her like a ton of bricks. A little over two months ago, she was in L.A. where she spent intimate time with Mark at Danny's beach house and a few times at Mark's home on the weekends. *Oh, my God! I have been impregnated by Mark. What will I tell Evan? What will I do?* she wondered. Evan forgave her when she admitted to the affair with Mark, but this was something Evan would not forgive her for. This was too much.

Anna was in shock for a few days after being told she was pregnant. She had no idea what this would mean for her marriage and what should she do about it. Should she have an abortion? Should she tell Evan? She had an even larger problem. Evan was sick and she did not know what was wrong with him. He had not gone to class for a week, which had never happened before. He had a bad cold and cough. He was also losing weight and looked gaunt. He insisted on going to the doctor alone. He told her he had a bad case of the flu and diarrhea, but Anna was not so sure. She sensed something much more serious but remained quiet. Whenever she tried to get him to visit a medical specialist, he became angry and told her to stay out of it. She could not understand why his behavior suddenly changed for the worse. Everything seem to be coming apart in Anna's life. She was pregnant, Evan was sick and the company she worked for was being sold and she could be out of a job in a few months.

CHAPTER

6

Zurich 1984

Else and Frederic had been trying to have a
baby for several years. This was their third try
at a successful pregnancy. There were minor
complications, but everything looked good so
far. Else was in her fourth month and happily
eating everything in sight. She had a weakness
for Lindt caramel ice cream. She ate a quart a
day. Frederic was beside himself with joy. He
was gleefully overwhelmed with the prospect of
having a healthy baby. He would return home
from work with fresh lilies and chocolates for
Else almost on a daily basis. He now believed
he would leave this world with an heir,
hopefully a son.

Frederic would make it a point to confer
with Else's doctors frequently by phone or he
would make unannounced visits to their offices
to make sure all was well with Else. She told
him it was not necessary and it was humiliating
when she visited her doctors and they all would

tell her, "Your husband was just here a few days ago." She laughed. "Frederic, I want you to promise me you will stop interfering with my doctors. They tolerate you because of of your prominence. Anyone else would probably be kicked out of the office."

Frederic laughed and agreed he should stay away for a while and allow them to do their jobs. "Sweetheart, I want this child so badly, it's all I think about day and night; I will finally have my own child," he said.

"Don't you mean we will have our own child?" she asked wryly.

"Oh yeah, I'm sorry, I misspoke," he laughed.

Frederic came skipping into the kitchen like a school boy on the playground as he unexpectedly gave Else a gentle kiss on the cheek and a small red box. She opened the box and there was a solid gold pacifier. "Oh my God, Frederic! It's beautiful, but the child cannot suck on this," she laughed.

"I know, I had it especially made as an heirloom we will keep forever." She shook her head from side to side and smiled at her overly excited husband. Else and Frederic had been debating what the name of the baby should be. If it was a girl, Else wanted to name the child Sofia after her mother's middle name. Frederic wanted to name the child Evan after his favorite uncle, who was killed in the war. They would sit up for hours after dinner over a glass of Chardonnay, discussing what to called the baby.

It was a beautiful winter morning with a stinging chill in the air. The cold air caused Else's nostrils to burn slightly as she covered her nose with the tip of her favorite scarf for warmth. A few minutes later she was comforted by the overwhelming aroma of the freshly brewed coffee that Mr. Schwartz made each morning at his family-owned coffee store, where they had roasted coffee since the 1880s. People from far and wide gathered at the store's front door before dawn each day to be among the first to enjoy the unique flavor of his

La Stanza coffee. Life was good and Else felt great for the first time in weeks as she walked briskly along Stanstad Plaza. She smiled as she thought about her last doctor's visit. The doctor said all was well and her bouts of stomach pain had stopped weeks ago.

She loved shopping at the Burke Market. It was one of the best outdoor markets in Zurich. She would buy her favorite carefully picked produce there each week. She smiled cheerfully when she saw Genie, the girl who sold the best avocados in Zurich. Genie greeted her as Else approached her stall. "Good morning, Frau Else," she said. Elsa tried to return her greeting, but the words never passed her lips as her tongue felt heavy and it was difficult to speak. She was suddenly jolted by the horrendous pain searing throughout her body as the bright sunlight became dimmer until she was left in total darkness. Her legs felt rubbery and no longer supported her body as dizziness overcame her and she collapsed onto the street. She could hear others yelling, but could not see anyone. "Somebody help her!" she heard a man's voice nearby. "Call the medics!" a woman screamed hysterically.

The tall, fair-haired woman's body crumpled to the ground as if she had been shot by a sniper hiding in a nearby building. She landed head first onto the red cobblestone street, knocking herself unconscious. The red apples, yellow onions and blueberries spilled from her shopping basket, rolling swiftly down the narrow hilly street like multicolored balls towards the rain gutter, before disappearing into the darkness. Most of the on-lookers stood frozen in time as they stared in silence at the woman's lanky frame lying on the street face up. The bright winter sun blanketed her face, eyes closed. She looked as if she was taking an afternoon nap as the blare of the approaching ambulance became louder.

The bright lights in the room hurt Else's eyes as she strained to regain her vision. Frederic was the first to yell out to the doctors, "My wife is awake, she's awake!" as two doctors and a nurse scampered to her bedside.

She had tremendous pain in her stomach and her only thoughts were of the baby.

"Doctor, how is my baby?" she asked anxiously.

"The baby appears to be well, Mrs. Bulon," said the doctor.

While the doctor spoke, she looked at Frederic for reassurance. He smiled and said, "You're going to be ok, sweetheart." But she knew he was not telling the truth. She could see it in his eyes as she relapsed into a state of depression and began crying. "Else, everything will be fine darling, I swear to you," Frederic said. She could still feel the baby, but something was not right.

Frederic knew from talking to the doctors in private there was a good chance the baby might not survive. The doctors insisted they were doing all that could be done for Else and the baby. Frederic would not accept their diagnosis. He was determined to have a baby, and preferably a boy. The doctors said there was some type of birth defect that would prevent the baby from growing and it would eventually die in the womb. Frederic's eyes teared up as he listened to a team of doctors who sounded as if all was hopeless. He got angry and accused the doctors of being lazy and not creative in their thinking.

A few days later he had Else moved to the Zurich Research Hospital where his best friend, Dr. Jamie Heinz, was the Chief Medical Officer and a brilliant doctor with a background in genetics. Frederic had been told by Jamie that certain medical trials on human stem cell research were in the early stages in Europe. Zurich Research Hospital was one of the leaders in the field. There had been successful human trials done on pregnant woman whose babies would not have a chance for survival under normal conditions. But with this new revolutionary stem cell process there was a possibility the genetic defects that would normally kill the baby could be reversed. This is what Frederic was hoping for.

The only problem was that this process was still considered illegal and was only used under strict conditions approved by the government. Frederic knew that the government would never approve of what he wanted to do. He knew there were successful trials but what was not widely known was the government trials were done on 120 pregnant women and only 6 of the babies survived the trials. Once that was revealed, the government did not allow any further trials on humans. There were too many unknowns surrounding the process. But Frederic was willing to take the risk if he could get Jamie's support. Frederic wanted to present his idea to Jamie to feel him out. He scheduled a lunch meeting for later in the week.

Jamie was a big, jovial man with a shocking lock of red hair that seemed to always need combing. Frederic would be amused whenever the two would see each other. For some reason Jamie would inevitably have food stains somewhere on his suit jacket, shirt, necktie or somewhere else. Frederic was convinced Jamie was born with a hole in his chin where his food would drip onto his clothing regardless of how much care he took to prevent it. Jamie was also insightful and at the same time could be reserved and mysterious. Frederic always felt, in spite of his old friend's jovial manner, there was something about him that was deep and dark. But he preferred to not give much thought to that type of speculation since he really needed Jamie now more than ever.

Frederic sat nervously in the restaurant waiting for Jamie. He rehearsed in his mind what he would say to Jamie, hoping to persuade him to help with Else's pregnancy. Jamie walked into the restaurant a few minutes after Frederic. They greeted each other with big bear hugs and much laughter as they teased each other about who had become the fattest since the last time they saw each other. They discussed work, family, and politics over several shots of Glenfiddich Scotch. Frederic knew that was Jamie's favorite scotch. He gave him a big bottle for Christmas a few years ago and Jamie never stopped thanking him for it. They enjoyed a huge meal and talked about getting together more often. The atmosphere suddenly changed when Jamie asked about Else.

"Frederic, you have not mentioned your lovely wife. I heard she was pregnant, is that true?"

"Yeah, it's true."

Frederic's smile faded as he looked away nervously to avoid Jamie's gaze.

"Is something wrong with Else?" Jamie asked.

"Yeah, that's one of the reasons I had to see you today, Jamie."

Jamie examined Frederic's reactions closely as he spoke. He sensed Frederic had something in mind that was very serious.

"Ok, let me hear it. I want to know everything, Frederic."

Frederic told him about his idea for using the stem cell procedure on Else. Jamie remained quiet until Frederic finished and gulped a double scotch before he spoke.

"You do realize I could lose my medical licenses and possibly go to jail if I do what you're asking?"

"Yes, I know, Jamie. If you say no, I will understand, but we have tried so hard to have a child and it never works out. Else and I agreed that if she does not have a successful pregnancy this time, we will not try again. Jamie, I want a child, please help me. You have three healthy kids and take it for granted. We want this child more than anything in the world," he pleaded.

Jamie sat quietly before speaking. "I will think about it and give you a call tomorrow. I have to sleep on this."

Jamie called Frederic early the next day and agreed to help with Else's pregnancy. Frederic was overjoyed and could not contain his enthusiasm and thanked Jamie profusely after telling him he loved him. When Jamie hung up the phone he thought more about the risks involved with the procedure. He also thought about the potential financial benefits he would gain if this went as planned.

Frederic raced over to the hospital to explain everything to Else, who was taking a nap when he arrived. The doctor suggested he wait until she awoke, but Frederic could not wait; he was too excited.

"Sweetheart! I have fantastic news."

Else looked at him, blurry eyed after her nap. For the first few seconds she was not sure what he was saying.

"Frederic, what do you want?" she asked.

"Jamie has agreed to work on a special protocol involving stem cells that we believe will help you and the baby."

"What do you mean? What are stem cells? You moved me here for some type of new medical experiment?" He told her initially he moved her because he did not like the doctors at the other hospital, and he wanted to make sure all medical options were explored.

"Sweetheart, we have a procedure that will help us have a normal, healthy baby."

"How do you know, Frederic?"

"I cannot tell you all the details, but Jamie and I are sure that it will work."

Else was not entirely sure about it, but she saw the look on his face whenever he mentioned the baby. She agreed to have the experimental procedure if it meant she could have a healthy child.

A few weeks later Jamie performed the procedure and all went well. Else had a healthy eight-pound baby boy months later. Frederic was ecstatic and could not contain himself. He really went over the top when the doctor told him it was a boy. He bought soccer balls, baseball gloves, bikes, and so on. "Frederic you're acting like a fool! The baby was just born six weeks ago. What are you doing?" Else asked, smiling. She knew this was the most important event in his life other than marrying her. He was an only child and in recent years he talked about not having any heirs. But now, his baby boy Evan would change all of that, he boasted.

Else asked him to explain the medical procedure that was used during her pregnancy.

He paused slightly before speaking. "Well, Jamie had to insert stem cells into your placenta to access the baby's body fluids that allowed for it to grow to a healthy state."

"Where did the stem cells come from, Frederic?"

"Sweetheart, it's very complicated and I do not want to bore you with medical details that will mean nothing to you. The only thing that matters now is you are well and we are the proud parents of little Evan Bulon." She agreed the baby was healthy, and that's all that mattered. But she wondered should she tell him about the bad dreams she'd been having since the baby was born. She decided not to, because Frederic was so happy. He seemed like the man she married years ago. The baby brought so much joy into their lives. They were like two kids with a new toy.

Several years later Frederic and Else moved to Paris. Evan was now a healthy young boy with a big appetite. The doctor said he was huge for his age and Frederic would get excited when the doctor would say such things. He knew his only boy was going to be special. Frederic's career was also blossoming and he became the Chief Executive Officer for one of the biggest companies in France. He was a multimillionaire and well known in business and political circles in Europe. Some questioned his business ethics, but others admired him for his business acumen. Life was good for Else and Frederic, and baby Evan was their dream come true.

Time passed swiftly and Evan became a preteen. He was a brilliant student with many academic honors. His parents were proud of their young son who held so much promise. Else would frequently brag to her neighbors about how accomplished Evan was and how ambitious his future plans were. He wanted to be a lawyer and go to college in America. Others would frequently comment on how happy she seemed and the positive energy that surrounded her.

But Else's smile and positive energy hid her sadness. She was still bothered by bad dreams during the night. They had become worse over the years and all involved Evan. She would wake up horribly afraid and confused. The dreams seemed to always be about something tragic happening to Evan, but she could never see clearly see what it was. It was not about him being hurt in an accident or anything like that, but something about who he really was. Her deep apprehension seemed to grow the older Evan became. The dreams had become more vivid. She never mentioned anything to Frederic because he would dismiss it and tell her to forget it, but she couldn't.

In spite of his success, Frederic was depressed. The time was fast approaching where he could no longer hide from Else what he had kept to himself since his birth. He dreaded the moment he would have to be honest with Else and tell her everything. Over the years he felt Else was suspicion about the birth, but since the baby was healthy, she never said much. Sometimes Frederic would notice Else staring at him with an inquisitive expression. It was as if she had a question for him, but was afraid to ask.

The next day he surprised Else with a beautiful handmade silk scarf and a Tiffany gold bracelet. "Oh my God! What's the occasion, Frederic? What did I do to deserve this? You must be up to something," she laughed.

"No sweetheart, it's just a token of my love for you. Let's enjoy a large glass of my special Merlot and talk after dinner." He gave his wife a big warm hug and sat in his favorite chair to read the newspaper while Else prepared dinner. He was apprehensive, but the evening was going well and he felt this was the night to tell her everything. Else was happy her husband was in such a great mood. She suspected he wanted to talk to her about something, but she did not know what. The gifts were a clue. Later after dinner, while relaxing in his favorite easy chair, he looked up from his newspaper, took off his reading glasses and took on a serious demeanor before he said anything to Else. She looked up from the table where she had been playing a crossword puzzle and somehow felt he wanted to share something with her. Something other than the normal chit chat they usually engaged in after dinner each night.

"Sweetheart, I have something to share with you about the medical procedure you had before Evan's birth."

"It's been over twelve years and I have often wondered about it. What do you want to tell me, Frederic?" she asked in a low, apprehensive voice.

"When Jamie reviewed your medical test results years ago, he discovered that the stem cell procedure he used to help your pregnancy was not going to work unless we found some other way to improve the process. Jamie learned about another technique from his travels to Germany that he thought could be used to help you deliver a healthy baby. He included that new technique when he treated you during your pregnancy. We saw immediate results and thought we were on the right track."

Frederic's voice slowly changed as he began speaking in a low, halting manner while hanging his head down as if he had a sudden fascination with the floor. "Jamie called me one night and told me he had disturbing news. He had made a shocking discovery about the stem cell procedure we used during your pregnancy. He said one of the unforeseen consequences of the treatment was when Evan reached puberty and become a young man he would suffer from a condition that could result in his early death. Evan is the carrier of an unknown virus that has no cure, and we know very little about it. The good news is that the virus is currently in a dormant state, but if it ever became active it would take his life."

He never looked at Else while he spoke. It was obvious to Else he was trying to avoid her stare. Else could no longer contain herself and interrupted him as he tried to continue speaking.

"My God! Frederic, what are you talking about? How does this virus become active and

what will it do to our child? Tell me, Frederic!"
she asked, near panic.

Frederic raised his head to face Else. His
face was drawn and lacked blood. He looked
like a ghost, he was so white. "Sweetheart, it
hurts me to tell you this, but you should know
the truth. The first time that Evan becomes
sexually active as a young man, it will be his
last. The virus will be release in his body and
will be no longer be dormant. Evan and his
partner's body will begin to reject all
nourishment and they will eventually die over a
matter of weeks once the condition appears.

It's all my fault, Else, but I wanted a baby so
badly. Jamie and I did not know this would
happen when we gave you the experimental
treatment." He fell to his knees, begging Else
for forgiveness. His hands covered his face as
he wept in agony. "Oh, God, please forgive me
sweetheart. I did what I thought was best. Can
you forgive me, Else? Please forgive me."

Else was incredulous as she listened to her
husband's unbelievable story. "How can you be
so sure about all of this, Frederic? How do you

know whether this is true? Jamie could have been lying about all of this," she said. "My heavens, this is a nightmare." She glared at Frederic with tears running down her face.

"Else, I have known Jamie all my life. He would never lie to me or tell me something wrong, especially with something as important as our desire to have a baby. I don't understand everything he did, but I would swear on a stack of bibles he was doing his best to help us, Else. Don't you believe that?"

Else remained quiet and gave no response to his question. She could not believe what she had just heard from the lips of her husband. After listening to Frederic's pleas for forgiveness, she became uncontrollably enraged.

"My God, Frederic! How could you do this to me and Evan? How could you? You are a monster!" she screamed out. She sprung from her chair and begin pounding him in the chest with both fists as she screamed in anguish. "Why? Why? You are a fucking FRANKENSTEIN! I hate you.

I knew something was wrong when I was pregnant. All those bad dreams, I knew they meant something." Frederic stood as his wife cried and asked him questions for which he had no answers. Else screamed at him, "WHEN ARE YOU GOING TO TELL EVAN? YOU SON OF A BITCH!"

Frederic responded in a quiet, whimpering voice. "I will tell him this afternoon after he gets home from school." His eyes were red from crying.

Else was so overcome she fainted and fell back onto the sofa. Frederic grabbed her by the waist and lifted her body off the sofa and caressed her for dear life as he cried out like a child begging for forgiveness. He held Else's body and supported her while she leaned against him like a lifeless rag doll. He revived her and gave her a sedative and carried her to the bedroom, where she slept the rest of the afternoon.

Frederic counted the hours before Evan would return from school. This would be the most important subject he'd ever discussed with his son and he was beyond apprehensive. He broke out in a rash and perspiration dripped from his forehead as he thought about what he would say to Evan.

Evan thought it was unusually quiet in the house. Else was usually painting one of her art pieces, listening to jazz and even talking on the phone while simultaneously smoking cigarettes. She was nowhere to be found. All was quiet today and the house seemed dark and gloomy for some reason. Evan could not figure it out. He felt something was wrong. Frederic met Evan in the hallway and asked him to follow him to the den.

"I need to talk to you about something very serious, son."

"What, dad?"

"There's something you should know now that you are almost 14 years old and becoming a young man."

Evan sat and stared curiously at his father. He wondered what was coming next as

Frederic began speaking. His dad looked worried, almost fearful, for some reason.

"Evan, I have dreaded this day since you were born. But I knew this day would come. Your mother had a difficult time when she was pregnant with you. She was very sick and there was a chance you would not survive. We were desperate for a solution. I asked your Uncle Jamie to try a new, unheard of medical procedure involving the use of human stem cells."

"Oh yeah, we studied about cells in biology at school."

"No, these cells are different. Most people knew very little about these particular type of cells when you were born. Your Uncle Jamie believed these cells could perform miraculous things, like help people with rare, untreatable diseases become well.

"Uncle Jamie used these cells to treat your mother when she was pregnant with you and the method he used work well, since you were born healthy and your mother and I thanked

God each night for giving us a child after so many failures. But I learned later that the procedure we used to guarantee a successful pregnancy had unforeseen circumstances that were not good."

"Like what, dad?" he asked, moving uncomfortably in his chair with a concerned look.

"You were born with an unheard of virus that took hold in your body at birth. Jamie ran all kinds of tests to determine what it was and where it came from. He was one of the world's foremost geneticists and he could not figure it out. We did learn some things, and none of them good. Uncle Jamie discovered that the virus destroys human organs over a period of weeks once it's activated from its dormant state in the human body."

"What do you mean, activated?" asked Evan.

"The virus will activate itself the first time you have intercourse with a woman. Both of you will become infected and die shortly afterwards. I was devastated when I discovered this. I just told your mother today for the first time, and she is in shock. I held this secret for many years hoping your Uncle Jamie would find a cure, but he never did. We had no luck son, and I'm terribly sorry."

Evan listened in a state of confusion. He stared at Frederic in raw fear before he spoke. His mouth was agape, eyes wide like saucers, his chest heaving under his argyle sweater and perspiration dripped heavily down his forehead.

"My God, dad! What does this all mean? Is there anything you can do to help me?" Evan suddenly seemed as if he was becoming dizzy and crumpled into his father's arms. He was shattered.

"No, son, I'm so sorry. Please forgive me." Frederic hugged his only son with all his strength as he cried heavily.

"What have you done to me, dad? My life is ruined forever," Evan said as he cried with a passion that caused Frederic to crumple to the floor holding on to his son for dear life.

Several months later, Else divorced Frederic and moved to Amsterdam and took Evan with her. Frederic eventually left Zurich and moved to Athens to continue his work. Else and Frederic remained cordial because they loved Evan and it was thought best to have some type of relationship on Evan's behalf. A few years later Evan left Holland to go abroad to America to continue his studies and pursue his dream of going to law school in America. His life forever changed.

CHAPTER

7

San Francisco 2014

Evan had taken a turn for the worse. He was bedridden and required 24-hour medical care. The company Anna worked for was sold and she would probably be laid off in a few months. She was pregnant and did not believe in abortion. Her world was crashing in on her with no relief in sight. Her biggest worry was Evan. The doctors could not determine what was wrong with him. He had undergone various tests, but nothing was promising and he seemed to get sicker by the day.

His hair had turned prematurely gray and his skin was ashen. The beautiful boyish face had been replaced by one filled with small red blotches covering most of his forehead. Those beautiful hazel eyes were now much darker and sat further back in his head. He did not look like the man she married over a year ago in Carmel. She was guilt ridden because of her pregnancy and the fact that Evan did not have a clue about her condition. She had nowhere to turn.

Anna received an unexpected text message from Simone. She was in L.A. and would be flying up to San Francisco and wanted to have what she called a much needed dinner meeting with Anna. She said she wanted to discuss something very important. Anna was in no mood to see Simone or anyone else. But for some reason she felt she should meet with her, and agreed to do so. Simone was not the type of person who would pop up out of nowhere without a good reason.

The next evening Simone walked into the restaurant at exactly 7:00 PM. Her demeanor was serious, as if she had a very clear purpose for being there. She greeted Anna with a brief embrace and a kiss on both cheeks in the Euro manner. Anna smiled and returned the two cheek kiss. After ordering drinks, the two began talking.

"It's so good to see you, Anna, and I'm happy we were able to get together. Thanks to you, I will always consider this our special place each time I'm in San Francisco," she smiled.

Anna smiled stiffly and shook her head in agreement. But there was something Anna was always curious about, and she decided to ask Simone.

"I know it's not my business, but why is it no one ever mentions Frederic's wife? I would have expected to see her at the wedding last year and thought it was odd she was not there."

Simone gave her a knowing smile before she said anything. "Frederic's wife Nina is a shut-in. Six months after they were married she came down with a crippling disease. She does not travel and prefers to be left alone. I only met her once and she did not seem particularly welcoming. Sometimes I felt Frederic was ashamed of her. Her name seldom came up in our conversations." Anna had her answer and felt there was nothing more to be said about her father-in-law's wife.

Simone looked carefully at Anna before speaking. "I need to share something very personal with you, Anna." Her expression and the tone of her voice signaled what she was about to say was not good. Anna knew this was not a trip Simone took because she happened to be in the area. She had a purpose that Anna feared she would soon discover. Simone reached across the table and held Anna's hand before she said anything. Her face slackened, her brow furrowed and her eyes darted about as if she were searching for a place to hide before she spoke. "I'm afraid I have bad news. I have incurable cancer, and my doctor says I don't have long to live."

Anna listened quietly to Simone's shocking news. She was surprised at her own reaction as her eyes moistened and slowly filled with tears. Simone ignored Anna's tears and continued speaking. Anna was not particularly close to Simone, but the notion that she was sitting across from someone whose life would soon end greatly upset her. Maybe because Evan was home critically ill and his future was uncertain. Simone said she'd made peace with herself and was prepared for whatever happened next, and there was no need for tears. Anna could not believe the way Simone spoke about her impending death as if she was talking about shopping or something much less serious. She seemed so casual about it.

Simone described herself as an agnostic. "I do not accept the notion of a deity or commit to any religious doctrine, but I do believe my soul will move to the next plane of existence when it leaves this earth," she said. Anna began to think Simone would be fine when she died. She'd never felt this way before when a friend or family member was nearing death. She believed Simone knew what the hereafter held for her. Anna's tears seemed almost unnecessary because of Simone's certainty about life after death. In a strange way, it gave Anna a feeling of comfort about death and what awaits all of mankind.

She studied Simone's face for clues as she tried to figure out the real reason Simone wanted to meet with her. She initially thought it was to inform her about her impending death from cancer. But she now felt it was something else. Neither spoke and remained quiet for several awkward moments as they pondered their private thoughts. Simone looked away from Anna's stare and gazed evasively at the floor before saying anything.

"Anna, I'm going to tell you the truth about the birth of your husband."

"What are you talking about? What do you mean the truth? I don't understand."

Anna's stomach churned and she suddenly felt nauseous. It was as if her body was preparing her for something unpleasant. When she was a little girl she would get this sensation when she got a rare spanking. She listened carefully as Simone spoke in a slow, deliberate manner.

"During the years before Evan was born, his parents were desperate to have a child. They tried twice before and each time it did not work out. Your father-in-law Frederic wanted a son desperately. He wanted an heir to the Bulon estate. When Else became pregnant with Evan, Frederic was determined that she would have a successful pregnancy, regardless of what it took.

Frederic's best friend was a man named Jamie Heinz. He was a brilliant geneticist and a medical doctor. He was also the Chief Medical Officer for the Zurich Hospital. Frederic begged and convinced Jamie to treat Else with a revolutionary medical technique involving the use of human stem cells. Jamie developed a never before tried medical procedure that resulted in Else giving birth to a healthy baby. Frederic was so happy he literally cried when Evan was born.

"But years later, Frederic received shocking news from Jamie. Jamie said he only recently discovered Evan was infected with an unknown virus that could result in his premature death as he grew older. Frederic was devastated; he was certain Jamie did everything proper in developing the medical protocol that was used on Else during her pregnancy. Jamie said he was shocked and felt responsible, since things did not go as planned. He swore to Frederic that he would find a way to save Evan's life before it was too late. Jamie confided to Frederic that one of the horrific side effects of the virus was as Evan grew older and became sexually active, he would unleash the dormant virus in his body. This would not only infect Evan but any partner he had sexual intercourse with. Frederic was traumatized after discovering this and for the next few years suffered from tremendous guilt. He decided to wait until Evan was older and could understand before he would tell him what he had learned from Jamie."

Anna was glued to her seat as she listened to this unbelievable story. Simone then asked Anna to brace herself before she continued.

"There was something about Jamie that Frederic did not know. Jamie was a gambler and a big risk taker. He was greedy and in debt. He owed thousands of dollars to a local crime syndicate and they wanted their money or threatened to take his life. Later that month he was approached by representatives from a German company that was also working on a revolutionary medical project involving stem cells. But their project was far more ambitious and mysterious. They were willing to pay Jamie thousands of dollars if he would use stem cells taken from a rare Australian mammal species and combine them with human stem cells that would be inserted into a pregnant human female.

Jamie made the deal and secretly agreed to introduced the human-animal stem cell combination into Else's placenta. The Germans told him the child would be virtually immune from most diseases that plague mankind and the protocol would have no adverse effects on the baby. Jamie became excited when they told him the medical patents would be worth millions if the experiment was successful. Jamie knew he could never tell Frederic about the deal because Frederic would never agree to such a horrible thing. But Jamie needed the money and he was in a precarious situation. He went into the lab early on a Sunday morning when it was closed and no one was there. He combined the animal and human cells, which were later inserted into Else's placenta during her regular medical appointment the following week. Else was totally unaware of what was taking place when he gave her a shot of what he described as high potency vitamins that would insure the health of the baby. Once that was done, he received a payment of $250,000 from the Germans. He used the money to pay off his debt to the crime syndicate.

A few years later my friend Marta, who worked for Jamie, called me late one night in tears. She was in charge of the medical records in Jamie's laboratory. She told me that Jamie had a small group of secret files that were locked away from everyone except Marta. He was a meticulous record keeper and documented all his work. He believed someday his hidden work would bring him great wealth whenever he decided to release his findings to the world. When Marta read the file on Else, she was horrified. She swore me to secrecy and told me the stem cells Jamie used on Else were taken from a rare Australian mammal called an Antec. During the mating season, the male Antec would engage in a marathon mating session with the female that could last up to 14 hours. When the mating session was over, the male dies, and the female survives. The male only mates once in its short life.

"One day Jamie received a confidential file by mistake from the German company. The file contained data which revealed what the Germans said years earlier about their medical protocol not harming the baby was not true. The file revealed that the stem cells which cause the male Antec to mate once and die were located in Evan's body. This was devastating. Jamie thought he had removed that particular cell family so it would not be included in the protocol he used on Else." Anna sat dumbfounded and couldn't speak as Simone continued with her incredible story.

"Jamie discovered Marta learned about the failed stem cell protocol used on the unsuspecting Else from reading his secret files. She had a master key which allowed her entry to any part of the laboratory, where she discovered the files. He panicked and begged her not to disclose it to anyone. He told Marta he had no idea it would fail and he would never forgive himself. Marta was not sure whether to believe him or not. She believed that he did not have the heart or the courage to tell Frederic what really happened, in spite of being his best friend. A few days later Marta's body was discovered in a dumpster in Crete. The body had been butchered and the parts burned to remove any evidence. No one was ever charged for the crime, but I will go to my grave believing that Jamie had Marta murdered. He was afraid she would tell others about the illegal stem cell protocol he used on Else, and the money he pocketed from the Germans."

When Simone revealed what happened to Marta, she became sad. There was an aura of grey around her as a single tear rolled down her cheek. Anna was moved emotionally when she witnessed Simone grieving. Simone was a person who rarely showed emotion, regardless of how bad or good something was. After a minute or so, Simone's lips quivered as the words from her mouth came out slowly, with some hesitance. "I must confess something to you, Anna. Marta was more than a friend to me. She was my lover. We had been together for years and I loved her dearly. I felt it was important that you know the full story. Once I die, the story of what really happened will die with me since Jamie and Marta are already dead." Anna was surprised at Simone's revelation, but she still had questions that needed answers.

"What happened to Jamie?"

"He began working feverishly to find a way to reverse the impact of the Antec stem cells in Evan's body. Jamie figured he had time to correct his mistake before Evan reached manhood. But he was not successful. He spent the next few years of his life filled with regret because of his inability to find a method to reverse the failure of his work. Late one evening after dinner his wife found him hanging from the rafters in the basement of their home. He committed suicide. He took the coward's way out."

Anna was aghast. "What kind of crazy story is this Simone? Do you expect me to believe this bullshit?"

"Anna, I know it sounds crazy and unbelievable, but all of it is sadly true. I'm concerned about your husband. How long has Evan been sick?"

"A couple of weeks, why?'

"I know this is personal, but I am assuming that you and your husband recently consummated your marriage."

"That's none of your business."

"I know, but I'm only trying to help you Anna. If you had consummated your marriage in the past, he would be dead by now."

Anna was afraid and confused. What Simone said had a ring of truth to it and it shocked and sickened her. She began crying and lowered her head before she answered Simone's question.

"My husband and I consummated our marriage two weeks ago....and... it was

beautiful. What does all this mean, Simone?"
She began weeping like a child.

"Anna, you should take a leave from work
and take care of your husband in his last days."

"There is something I still do not
understand, Simone. Why would Jamie lie and
tell Frederic that Evan had a rare, unknown
virus? What was he trying to do?"

"Jamie lied to Frederic from the beginning
about Evan having an unknown virus. The
story was just a delaying tactic to give him time
to find a solution to the Antec cells in Evan's
body, which was the real tragedy. When Jamie
discovered his mistake, Evan was already
twelve years old and would be entering puberty
in a few years, and Jamie was desperate to find
a solution.

He could not tell Frederic what he had
actually done to Else when he treated her
during her pregnancy years earlier. But he was
able to convince Frederic that the phony virus
story was true. Jamie also knew Frederic would
share the same story with Evan as he grew
older. He figured the phony virus story would

hopefully prevent Evan from any sexual activity until he could find an answer to the Antec cells inside Evan's body. He never did. Frederic and Evan never knew the actual truth. Evan spent his young life hiding what he thought was a horrible secret, which caused him great depression and fear. He believed he would be putting his life and the life of any female partner in danger if their relationship ever became intimate.

"The truth is that the only person in mortal danger was your husband, because of the Ante stem cells in his body. He will soon die if you consummated your marriage a few weeks ago. I'm sorry, Anna."

"Goddamn it! Simone. What kind of people are these? Why would they do this? Please tell me," she pleaded.

"Anna you must understand that Jamie was driven by greed and a massive ego. Frederic was desperate to have a healthy child. Jamie and Frederic gambled that they could develop the science which would guarantee a healthy baby, in spite of what mother nature decided.

They were only partially right. They never could have imagined the effect the Antec cells would have on poor Evan."

Anna was in a state of controlled panic as she tried to understand what she was told by Simone. She did not want to believe anything she heard, but certain things made sense the more she thought about it. She sat quietly reflecting while Simone said nothing and allowed Anna to immerse herself in thought. *If what she said is true, it would explain why Evan spent a year trying to avoid consummating our marriage up until two weeks ago, when we finally made love and he became seriously ill. Evan must have falsely believed he would infect me by consummating our marriage, thinking it would result in his death and mine. My God! He wanted me dead also, and for some reason it did not seem to matter to him.* She was confused and angry. *Why would he want to harm me?* she wondered.

Anna composed herself and told Simone that this entire story was too much to handle and she had to leave. She staggered out of the restaurant like someone who was drunk. She stopped outside and sat on a park bench to calm down and collect herself before going home. Anna left Simone sitting alone in the restaurant. They never said goodbye. Simone was not angry; she understood Anna's reaction to what she felt compelled to tell her. They never spoke again and Simone died three weeks later in her native Romania.

CHAPTER

8

Anna took a leave from work as Evan's condition became worse. Her days were filled with fear and uncertainty. She still had not recovered from her meeting with Simone and what she was told about Evan's birth. The fact that she was eight weeks pregnant was taking its toll, and Evan had no idea she was pregnant with the child of another man. He was so sick he would not understand. He was losing his cognitive abilities. His eyes were glassy with that faraway look; she was not sure he recognized her anymore.

She spent most of her time helping the home nurse take care of him. During the evening she would play his favorite Keiko Matsui jazz cd. He would usually fall asleep listening to the melodic ethereal sounds of the music with tubes coming out of his body and an oxygen mask covering his once handsome face. She was heartbroken as she sat quietly next to his bed while he slept, heavily medicated. She cried nightly because the person she loved more than life itself was no longer there. Anna's cell phone rang at 2:00 A. M. in the morning. She knew late night phone calls were usually bad news. She grabbed her cell phone and answered.

"Hello."

"Hello Anna, it's Frederic, how are you?"

"I'm fine, but its late."

"I apologize for calling so late, but I heard that Evan was very sick. Is that true?"

She was not sure what to say since she promised Evan she would not let his father know he was sick. She wondered how he knew, but remembered she told Else a week ago and she must have told Frederic. Anna was not really angry with Else because she also felt that Frederic should know; after all he was Evan's father.

"Yes, he's sick and it does not look good."

"I will catch a flight to San Francisco and we will be arriving tomorrow evening. Else will be traveling with me. Please have someone pick us up at the airport. I will see you tomorrow, Anna. Goodbye."

Frederic and Else could not believe how their only child had wasted away and no longer recognized either of them. Else broke into tears and caressed Evan as she cried uncontrollably. Frederic was overcome when he saw his son lying in bed almost lifeless. He was visibly shaken, but there was something Anna noticed. Neither asked many details about Evan's illness. Normally relatives would want to know every detail and circumstance surrounding a son who was near death.

This confirmed in Anna's mind what Simone told her was true. Frederic and Else thought they knew what caused his illness. They believed the lie that Jamie told Frederic years ago about Evan being born with some type of imaginary virus. What Frederic and Else did not know was the truth. Evan's illness was the result of the stem cells from the Australian mammal that Jamie inserted into Else's placenta when she was pregnant with Evan. Anna was in a state of disbelief when she thought about the whole situation. It seemed so unbelievable and she could never tell anyone the truth, because they would probably think she was crazy.

She prepared dinner each night for her father and mother-in-law. She knew if Evan was well he would enjoy the idea of Anna trying her new California cuisine dishes on his parents to show off her culinary talent. It was the only happy thought she'd had in weeks.

Frederic seem to have an unusual interest in Anna's health. "Anna, I understand that you are really into physical fitness, you certainly look great."

"Yeah Anna, I wish I could look as trim and vibrant as you do," Else commented. "But I read somewhere that even though one might look to be in good shape, sometimes serious medical issues may be hidden," she said.

"Tell me Anna, how is your health and when was the last time you had a good check-up?" Frederic asked.

"I just visited my doctor a few weeks ago and I'm in excellent health," Anna replied.

Frederic looked at Anna closely as if he was looking for something specific. Anna knew what he was looking for. He was trying to determine whether she had been infected by the imaginary virus that Evan carried and wondered why she was not seriously ill like Evan. Anna knew he was perplexed about her obvious good health and his son's imminent death.

When the polite but tense exchange was over, Anna decided to brighten up the evening. She surprised them by serving hot mango tea with sassafras root. Evan told her once that whenever there was a feeling of discomfort and edginess amongst the family, Else would serve her special tea and all would soon be better.

When Anna served them tea, Else's face lit up like a child who had found her lost toy. She had a look of sheer pleasure as she took her first sip of tea. "This is delicious Anna! What a great surprise," she grinned. Frederic was also smiling which seemed almost unnatural, Anna thought. The tea seemed to serve as an elixir that put them in a relaxed almost festive mood in spite of the reality of Evan lying just feet away in the bedroom near death. Shortly afterwards, Anna left them alone and wished them a good night.

"OH NO! OH NO! The loud scream echoed throughout the house. Anna jumped from her bed and raced to the bedroom where Evan slept. As soon as she entered the room she saw Frederic standing over Evan's bed with his hands over his face, sobbing like a child. He got up earlier to check on Evan and discovered he had passed away during the night. Else stumbled into the room half asleep, staggering toward Frederic, where they embraced and slowly slid to the floor in each other's arms in pain and grief.

"OUR BABY IS GONE! LORD HELP US!" Anna knew this night was coming and she held up better than the two of them. She was horribly crushed and cried as she hugged Evan. His body was cold and stiff, but she knew his spirit was no longer on this plane. For some reason the words Simone shared with her about death seem to console her. Evan had moved on to another level of existence and he would be fine. Her tears were many, but she felt sure he would be fine.

Evan's memorial service was held on a beautiful autumn morning. He was not religious, but requested his body be cremated and his ashes spread over the ocean. Anna and a small group of family and friends took a boat across the bay to the entrance to the Golden Gate Bridge. She released his pale gray ashes into the wind and watched as they drifted over the cold blue water disappearing into the Pacific. Anna was relieved because she had followed her husband's wishes to the end. A small group of mourners gathered at Anna's home to sit and reflect on the day's events. Some had come from out of town and felt a need to grieve and commiserate with each other.

Anna watched Frederic and Else closely and could tell that they wanted to talk with her about something in private. She would see them stealing glances at her while socializing with others in the room. It was obvious that they had something on their minds. After everyone left for home, Anna invited Else and Frederic to have a late brunch at her favorite restaurant in Berkeley. They all agreed it was a good idea to escape the house, because a pall of sadness had enveloped the house since Evan's death.

The three of them drove over to Anna's favorite restaurant on Telegraph Avenue. She loved the area because of the many places to eat and shop. Else and Frederic sat in the backseat of the car and remained quiet. They both seemed to be in a melancholy mood. They were obviously still grieving, but seemed better since leaving the house and enjoying the beautiful day. After a while Else even told one of her dirty jokes about a man and a chicken. Anna and Else laughed out loud but Frederic only smiled slightly. Maybe he did not get the joke, Anna thought. Anna entered the restaurant and greeted her favorite waiter Reynaldo, who gave her a big smile.

"Hola! Anna, how are you?'

"Hola! Reynaldo, it's good to see you."

He escorted the three of them to one of the best locations in the restaurant. The mood changed quickly as the three of them took their seats. The tension between them was palpable. They knew this was the time and place to be honest and truthful with each other. The time for secrets and lies was over. Frederic spoke first. "Anna you might have a hard time with what I am about to say, but Evan is gone and you need to know certain things. I feel I owe it to you. I know we have not been close, but there were reasons for my behavior.

Many years ago Else and I were desperate to have a baby after several failed attempts. We were about to give up until I heard about an unusual medical procedure using human stem cells to help insure a healthy pregnancy. My best friend Dr. Jamie Heinz was one of the world's best research geneticists. He agreed to try the stem cell process on Else and I assisted him. Five months later, Else delivered a healthy eight-pound baby boy." Anna sat quietly as she listened carefully to Frederic's story. Else said nothing and spent her time staring at the floor as Frederic continued.

"A few years later I was given horrible news by Jamie. He told me that Evan was the carrier of a dangerous, unknown virus. I was heartbroken. I eventually had to tell Else and Evan since neither of them knew about the virus at that time. Once I told them, they were devastated. But that was not the worst part. Jamie said if Evan ever had intimate relations with a woman the virus in his body would change from a dormant state to an active one and he and his partner would certainly die after intercourse. This was a terrible secret that Evan carried all his life. A secret he could never tell anyone. When he met you and fell in love I was horrified because I knew if the two of you became intimate, it could be fatal for you and Evan. This is why I tried my best to discourage Evan from marrying you." Anna said nothing as she listened to Frederic.

"Do you understand what I'm telling you, Anna?"

Anna sat motionless before she spoke. "Yeah, I do. But I'm afraid I also have some bad news to share with you."

"What do you mean?"

"I knew about the virus you believed Evan had. You also think that is what killed him. You were wrong. Jamie was a deceitful man who lied to you about this supposed virus years ago. He made the whole thing up. It was true that Evan would die the first time he had sex, but it was not because of some virus that Jamie accidentally discovered. What killed Evan was the combination of human stem cells and stem cells taken from an Australian mammal called an Antec. The man you thought was your good friend, Dr. Jamie Heinz, combined the two stem cell groups without your knowledge because he was in a desperate need of money. After Else was treated with the stem cell combination he was paid $250,000 dollars by a German company he had made a deal with. He agreed secretly to include the Antec animal cells into Else's body while she was pregnant. The treatment resulted in a successful pregnancy, but there was something you did not know. The combined stem cells infected Evan with a condition that would guarantee his death the first time he had sex with a woman. This same condition existed in the animal world, where the male Antec would mate with the female only one time for up to 14 hours and die afterwards.

"The first and only time Evan and I made love was his last. His illness and eventual death followed shortly afterwards. This is the real reason Evan died. The same genetic marker that existed in Evan's body was found in the Antec. He never knew what really happened to him, nor did his doctors. He died thinking that he was sick because of the story you told him as a boy about him having this imaginary virus that Jamie convinced you was real. It was all a lie and my beautiful husband's life was predetermined before he was born. You are partially responsible, Frederic, even though I know your intentions were good. The tragedy was that if it was not for the introduction of the Antec stem cells into the fetus while Else was pregnant, the baby would have been born healthy without the curse of the Antec mammal, which resulted in his death. "

Frederic looked as if he had seen a ghost when Anna finished speaking as the blood drained from his face. "What in the hell are you talking about, Anna? Who told you these things?" he asked. He was visibly shaken as his hands trembled violently and his face turned red. He was perspiring heavily and for some reason his glasses fogged up as he took them off to clean them using a small portion of the white linen tablecloth that covered the table. He looked as if he was about to have a stroke as his breathing became heavy as if he had just completed a marathon. "I do not believe any of this bullshit! Do you hear me, Anna?" His voice raised in anger and his eyes filled with rage. The waiter looked in their direction with a look of concern as other diners snuck curious glances at the table without wanting to appear intrusive.

Else listened and said nothing, but the expression on her face was wrathful. The veins in her long neck were bulging and her face was contorted in a disturbing frown. She was trembling and rubbing her hands as if she had a rash. She had a strong sense of dread about her. Anna became frightened as she looked at Else and wondered what she was thinking. She asked Frederic to calm down as she explained how she knew about Evan's birth. She did not tell him the original source for the story (Simone's friend Marta) but she did tell him about her meeting with Simone, who was now dead.

She provided numerous details about Jamie's personal life with his money problems and his greed. Frederic knew certain things were true. He also knew Jamie had been contacted by a German company for some exotic stem cell project, but Jamie told Frederic that he turned them down and said he was not interested in any type of partnership with the Germans. He obviously lied to Frederic. As the truth became more apparent to Frederic, he slumped in his chair, bowed his head and wept silently. He seemed to accept the fact that Anna was telling the truth.

She felt sorry for him and was about to comfort him when the next thing she remembered was the loud shrieking sound coming from Else as she jumped up from the table, screaming at Frederic, "YOU KILLED MY CHILD! YOU SON OF A BITCH!" Anna quickly stood up from the table to try and console Else. She only remembered the blurred motion of Else's blue dress moving with the speed of a cheetah as she plunged one of the steak knives from her silverware setting into his chest. The other customers stared in disbelief as he clutched his chest and looked at Else in horror. He tried to fend her off but her attack was swift, powerful and unexpected. She continued stabbing him until the waiter and another customer pulled her off of Frederic and took her away screaming.

There were screams for help by other customers who witnessed the brutal attack. Some ran for safety out of the restaurant into the street and called the police. Anna was weak with fear and trembling as she somehow ended up on the floor under the table during the commotion. When it was over she looked up from beneath the table to see Frederic's body still sitting in the chair. His upper body was bent over the table as if he was taking an afternoon nap, with his head resting on his dinner plate as dark red blood pooled onto the snow white table cloth with the gold trimmings. His still open dead eyes stared at Anna as she rose from under the table. A frozen expression of surprise was permanently imprinted on his face as life drained from his limp body. Frederic was dead.

In the weeks that followed Anna had an overwhelming desire to run and hide from everything and everybody. The world she thought she knew and understood was no longer real. What she desired more than anything was to be left alone. She needed time to reflect and sort things out. Her life had changed radically in such a short period. Her husband was gone and Frederic and Simone were dead. Else was in the Napa Hospital for the Criminally Insane. Anna visited her a few times and she was convinced Else was not insane, but went into a temporary rage when she realized her only child had been sacrificed by a greedy, arrogant individual who did it for money. Her anger at Frederic was probably misdirected, since it was Jamie who actually lied and deceived her and Frederic, but she could not control her actions that day and Frederic was the innocent victim.

She now believed God had not planned for her and Frederic to have a baby and they paid the price for tampering with nature. Sometimes it was best to leave certain things alone, she told Anna. Anna promised she would visit her often and write. The two of them developed a bond from the beginning and Anna would always see Else as the bawdy freewheeling spirit she met in Carmel on her wedding day eighteen months ago.

Hollywood, California

Mark was very busy in his office and his psychiatry practice was growing by leaps and bounds. It seemed that every major celebrity in

Hollywood wanted a session with him. In the past he prided himself on having a small boutique practice with a select group of patients. But now he was receiving calls from every major A list star in L.A. and he was not sure why. He was becoming uncomfortable with his rapidly growing practice, but had to admit the economics for such a practice were very appealing. His income had grown over 100% in recent months.

Sometimes during quiet moments, he would think about Anna. She left Los Angeles months ago and returned to the Bay Area. He was sure she would forget about him when she returned to her husband and resumed her life. But he was also sure he would not forget Anna. They had spent great moments together and for the first time he believed if he gave himself half a chance he could fall in love with her. He sometimes wondered what was it about her that touched something inside of him that was deep and sincere. He would quickly stop those thoughts because he knew it was improbable, if not impossible, that he would see the woman from the foggy city again.

Anna was back at work and there were big changes in the company. They had begun downsizing and several of her friends were no longer there. She was now four months pregnant and showing. Everyone assumed the father was Evan. All of her colleagues were overly sympathetic about Evan's death and Anna was beginning to feel like a victim. They treated her as if she had been diagnosed with cancer. Even Helen Duson, who was the CEO and the biggest bitch in the company, came to her office personally to reassure her that she would not be laid off. She even shed a corporate tear while she stared at Anna's stomach. Anna did not know whether to laugh or cry.

Evan's death and her pregnancy forced her to re-evaluate her life and determine what was important to her. To lose Evan so quickly was a sad but important lesson on how fleeting life can be. She wondered whether being a Vice President in a software company was who she really was. The only thing she was certain about was having the baby and raising it with all the love she could give it.

Anna spent the weekend packing up Evan's clothes, deciding to give them to the local Goodwill. She knew keeping personal items would depress her and it was important that she begin her new life and not spend time looking back. She was about to put his brown suede jacket in a bag and an envelope fell from the pocket to the floor with her name on it. It was odd to see a plain white envelope with Anna written on the front in Evan's handwriting. She opened the one-page letter and read it.

My Love,

I hope you are still alive to read this letter. I'm sorry for the evil I have brought upon you and I hope you will believe me when I tell you that my love for you was deep and profound. All of my life, I was plagued with this evil virus that prevented me from having a normal intimate relationship. I knew I should not have married you because the consummation of our marriage would have ended in both our deaths. I took a chance and married you hoping that my father or someone could help me with finding a cure for the virus I've had since birth. My father and I would fight about my marriage to you because he thought it was unfair to you and he was right. When you were in Los Angeles, I decided that the only fair thing for me to do was to take my own life and allow for you to go on without me. But when you told me about the affair with Mark, my love for you turned to intense hatred. I felt betrayed because you shared your love with another man even though you never shared it with me, your husband. I only had revenge on my mind the night we made love for the first time and finally consummated our marriage. I knew that death would claim us both after that night, but I also knew that in death we would both be together forever. Please forgive me. Evan.

Anna was speechless as the one-page letter fell to the floor from her now limp hands. She sat shakily on the sofa and put her trembling hands to her forehead, which was damp with perspiration. She could not believe what she read. To maintain her sanity, she had to say her thoughts aloud. "Evan consummated our marriage not because he loved me at the time, but because he hated me and wanted me to die like he knew he would, but not for the reason he thought. My God! He never knew the reason he died was because of the Antec stem cells in his body, not because of some imaginary virus. Jesus! My husband made love to me thinking I would die. What kind of fucked up world is this?" She suddenly felt weak and took her last dose of anti-depressant medication and went to bed. She did not want to face any more of life's ugly realities. After a while she fell into a deep sleep after a long, horrendous day, and looked forward to tomorrow for whatever it might bring. But tonight she only wanted to escape.

The next day would be better, because she would see her parents. They had been very supportive since Evan's death. Neither of them knew about the baby. She would make it a point to wear loose clothing the few times she saw her parents. Once her mom jokingly said, "Sweetheart your cheeks are so full, you look just like I did when I was pregnant with you, ha ha." Anna smiled and did not say much. Her mom was good at picking up on secrets as she stared at Anna with a quizzical look. Anna wanted to wait before she told her parents, since she wanted them to know their new grandchild would not be Evan's. It was becoming harder to hide it because it was only a matter of time before they knew. But she wanted to wait for the right time before she said anything.

It had been five months and Anna felt she should set things right by telling Mark about the baby. She called him early Sunday morning. For some reason the cool rainy day caused her to have sweet thoughts about him, and she wanted to hear his voice.

"Hello."

"Hi Mark, it's me, Anna."

"Hi Anna, this is a nice surprise, how are you?'

"I'm well, but my life has taken some serious turns since I saw you last."

"I know, I heard about you losing your husband. Madison told Danny and he mentioned it to me. I'm truly sorry, Anna. If there's anything I can do, please let me know. I wanted to call you when I heard about your husband but I was not sure if it was appropriate. I'm so happy to hear from you."

"It's good to hear your voice also, Mark. What's new in your life?"

"My practice is going gangbusters and I'm very busy. I have become the new 'it' guy when you need a therapist in Hollywood," he laughed. "I can't believe it since I'm not doing anything different. I guess it's just fool's luck."

They laughed as he told her some of the unusual clients he now had and how whacked out their personal lives were.

"What about you, Anna? Anything new or exciting?"

"Well, yes, there is."

"Tell me about it. Is it something you need advice on?"

"Maybe."

"What is it?"

"I'm pregnant."

"What! That's great Anna, congratulations. Your husband, bless his soul, went to the grave and left you a part of him that you will always have. That's beautiful."

"Not really, Mark, the baby does not belong to my husband."

"What do you mean?"

"Mark, the baby is yours."

There was silence on the other end of the phone. "Mark, are you still there?"

"This is unbelievable! I don't know what to say or how to act. My knees are shaking and I suddenly have to pee. Are you sure, Anna?"

"Yes, I am."

"I'm so happy, this is a miracle. WOW! This is shocking, but it's also a blessing."

Anna was moved to tears as she listened carefully to his every word. She held a deep fear that he would reject her and the baby. After all, he was a single Hollywood bachelor who had never been married or had kids. She assumed he would run away as fast as his feet could carry him. She could not believe how happy he seemed to be about her pregnancy. He wanted to see Anna as soon as possible. They talked for three hours non-stop about what this would mean for them. Anna had strong feelings for Mark. She had acknowledged it to herself after their first night together at Danny's beach house. But she knew a serious relationship was not possible at that time because she loved her husband and suffered tremendous guilt after that night.

They both admitted they were a little fearful about what the pregnancy would mean. Did it mean they are in love? Should they get married? Was it too soon for such an important step? The baby would change everything and they agreed being together would be the right thing to do. Mark knew how he felt about Anna after spending months thinking about her, and he was ready for the next stage of his life to begin. When he told her she was never far from his thoughts, she could hear the sincerity in his voice. She knew this man had strong feelings for her.

Mark was flying up from L.A. in a week and they would spend the weekend together in San Francisco. He got a room at the Fairmont Hotel and Anna joined him. She was uncomfortable about having him visit her home, and he understood. It was too soon after Evan's death. She was surprised at how excited she became when she thought about spending time with Mark. For the first time since Evan's death she had something to look forward to. In spite of her excitement, her emotional state was like a giant roller coaster. She would be emotionally up one day and terribly down the next. Mark told her that was to be expected after losing her husband.

Mark arrived in San Francisco early Friday evening and called Anna as soon as he checked into the hotel. She drove across the Bay Bridge to the hotel later that night. She had packed her overnight bag and was filled with anticipation. She had not seen Mark since the summer and for some reason it seemed like a long time. She wondered whether he would have second thoughts when he saw her and the reality of her pregnancy sunk in. *I better get that type of crazy thinking out of my head,* she concluded.

She felt a sense of guilt as she walked quickly across the thickly carpeted lobby of the Fairmont. She imagined everyone in the hotel was staring at her and thinking bad things about her. She soon regained her composure and realized how silly it was to have such thoughts. It was so ridiculous she could not stop laughing as she entered the hotel elevator. There was only one other person in the elevator and he stared at Anna as she stepped in. He probably thought she was one of those weird people in San Francisco he'd heard about as he watched her laughing to herself.

Mark opened the door and gave Anna a kiss that made her head spin. "It's great to see you, Anna," he gushed as he embraced her warmly.

His arms felt strong and reassuring as he held her. It was almost like the feeling she would get as a little girl when her dad would hold her when she was afraid of something. It was good to be in his arms again, but she felt trapped in a whirlwind of confusing and contradictory emotions. She had lost her husband who she loved. It was too early to get even think about getting into a serious relationship with anyone. However, when she saw Mark, she felt helpless.

Any confusion or contradiction seem to melt away while she sat with him in front of the fireplace nursing a glass of Chardonnay. He had a way of saying things that seemed to put her in a state of serenity. The night they spent at Danny's beach house was something she could never forget. The way he explained how relationships evolve between people and how it takes work to make them successful. What he said was not earth shaking, but the manner and simplicity he used in making his points had an everlasting impact on her.

Mark sipped his wine and looked at Anna with a smile that exuded a warmth and closeness that was almost palpable. Anna could literally feel the energy from him and it was unbelievably exciting.

"Tell me all about the baby. Have you thought about a name? Is it a boy or girl?" he asked.

"Whoa their partner, hold your horses, not so fast," Anna laughingly said. She could not believe how excited he was and how he seems to be so relaxed about the whole situation. She still had things she was not sure about, but she knew he was a good man and someone she wanted to be with. They spent the weekend discussing how they should handle their relationship. Should they get married now that the baby was coming? Should they move in together? Where should they live? He still lived in L.A., and she in the Bay Area. How would it look for her to be seriously involved with Mark after such a short time since Evan's death? Anna wondered how she would explain Mark to her parents once she told them about the baby.

Sometimes when she was alone, she would suffer periods of depression in searching for answers, complicated by loyalty, guilt and confusion. Mark helped her to navigate her emotions and concerns. Their relationship would be a monumental change for both of them. Anna decided she would move to L.A. and live with Mark. She felt that it would be wiser since he had his practice there and she was no longer sure she wanted to remain with Pallas Software. She also wanted to be with Mark. The baby was coming soon, which would represent a new start in life for her. She leased her home in Albany and moved to L.A.

Weeks later, Anna and Mark were busy planning for the baby. She called her parents and finally told them about Mark and her pregnancy. Her dad was not very happy about it, but seemed to accept something he had no control over. Anna's mother was more enthusiastic and never cast any judgement about this new and unexpected event. After Anna explained everything her mother seem to be excited about the prospect of a grandchild. "This is not what your father and I expected, but I am happy for you sweetheart. You have experienced a lot of heartbreak in the past year and I have not seen you this happy since your wedding. Are you and Mark thinking about marriage yet?"

"Mom, we will decide when the time is right."

"But what about the baby? The baby will need a mother and father; don't you think?"

"The baby will have a mother and father, Mark and I," she laughed.

She knew her mother wanted them to be married, but that was no longer a major requirement for Anna and Mark. They believed their happiness was based around their obvious love for one another and the baby. Marriage was a formality, if they ever decided to do so.

Mark had never mentioned his old girlfriend Merritt. Their relationship was in the past and he felt there was no need to tell Anna. But she had become a problem. Merritt was making unwanted phone calls to Mark even after he changed his cell number three times. They broke up months ago, but she insisted on trying to restart the relationship by wanting to see him. He made it clear that he had no longer had an interest in her. It didn't work because she began to show up at his office uninvited and would not leave until he saw her.

Merritt Blum was a beautiful woman with a large ego. She vowed she would not allow Mark to drop her like a hot potato. She always got what she wanted in life. Her father owned the largest and most successful real estate empire in Southern California and she was very rich. When they were dating, Mark would tell her she was the most exciting women he had ever met and was always surprised that a beautiful woman like Merritt would fall for a guy like him. He would jokingly say he was not 6'4" like her former boyfriend and he was not a wealthy entrepreneur. She would tell him it was his heart that captured her. But now she knew someone else was the object of his affection. She wanted Mark back and anyone who stood in her way or tried to keep her from him would be in serious trouble. Merritt considered Mark her man, even though he no longer felt that way. For the first time in her life she could not have what she so desperately wanted.

Merritt heard that Mark was involved with a woman from San Francisco who was living at his home in L.A. But when she heard that this woman was pregnant with his child she nearly had a seizure in Starbucks when her friend Sissy told her. The idea that Mark had impregnated a woman and she was living with him kept Merritt up at night. She fell into a state of depression the more she thought about Mark with this Anna bitch. She was losing weight and no longer left her Beverly Hills home. She stared at old photos of her and Mark together in the Caribbean and other places they had traveled together in the past. She hired a private investigator to keep track of all his activities. Most of all, she wanted to know about this Anna woman she believed seduced Mark. Merritt thought to herself, *"This bitch must have used her body to trap Mark. He belongs to me and I will not rest until I get him back and move this bitch out of his life for good."*

Anna had gained 30 pounds and spent her time preparing for the arrival of the baby. Mark could not wait to get home from his office each day to see her. He would routinely give her a big wet kiss on the lips followed by an even bigger kiss on her stomach. They both got a real kick out of the new routine, which ended in crazy laughter like two kids waiting anxiously for their soon to be delivered surprise. Anna was happy although she still suffered bouts of depression from time to time. They spent weekends at the beach, going to movies, and taking Lamaze classes. But what she enjoyed more than anything was sitting up at night with Mark just talking about all kinds of interesting topics. She found him fascinating and was always a willing student as she sat in rapt attention and listened to his views on one topic or another.

Mark was becoming nervous about the crazy antics of Merritt. He knew she had someone following him, and she still would come by his office even though he pleaded for her to stop. He now believed things had gotten out of hand and he needed to tell Anna about Merritt. He was so happy about his relationship with Anna and the idea of the arrogant and spiteful Merritt interfering would not be tolerated. He called his lawyer Ted Faulk and discussed getting a court order to keep Merritt away from him and Anna. Ted agreed to do so ASAP.

Anna prepared dinner using a recipe she had gotten from one of her new Persian neighbors, who told her it was the top dish in all of the best restaurants in Teheran. She spent the entire afternoon going from one market to the other to get the spices and other items she needed to prepare a special dinner for Mark. After several hours of following the recipe meticulously, she finished dinner and was proud of her accomplishment as soon as she tasted the first bite of lamb. She could not wait until he got home so she could surprise him with her new culinary creation.

Anna knew something was wrong as soon as he entered the house. He gave her a quick kiss and went to take a shower before dinner. There was no kiss on her stomach for the baby. *He's never done that before,* she thought. She did not ask what was wrong. She had learned it was best to wait until he told her, which she was sure he would. Mark loved her new dinner dish, but she felt for some reason he was not all there. She could tell he was not really paying attention as she enthusiastically shared the fun she'd had shopping at all the exotic markets she discovered in L.A.

"I have something to tell you, Anna."

"What, honey?"

"I dated a woman a while back who has returned to haunt me."

"What are you talking about, Mark? What woman?"

"Her name is Merritt Blum and she is well known here in L.A. She is a rich, spoiled brat who has been harassing me since she heard you and I were together. I broke up with her before I met you. She is not a good person. She is vindictive and hateful, and she could be trouble."

"What kind of trouble?"

"I don't know, but she is crazy, and as a psychiatrist I do not use that term loosely. Something is wrong with her and I need to figure out how to deal with her."

Anna did not know what to think. She had never seen Mark act this way before. He seemed worried and confused. She was fearful and was not sure what to think. Neither of them slept well that night. Anna felt vulnerable with the baby coming and now this woman who could be trouble.

Mark knew something was strange because the late model BMW had followed him for the past ten miles. He drove along the hillside road to his home and the car followed closely. He made an abrupt left turn away from his neighborhood and the BMW continued close behind him. He sped up and the other car sped up. He was afraid because he had no idea who it was and why they were following him. He slowed down to try and get a look at the driver, but it was almost dark and he could not tell who it was. The traffic light turned red as he watched the dark colored BMW creep closer to his rear bumper. Mark hit the gas and took off as the light changed to green, followed by the BMW. He grabbed his cell phone and was about to call the police when he saw the BMW right next to him on the driver's side. He was horrified because this was a two-way road and the BMW was in the wrong lane. An oncoming car would have probably hit both of them. He suddenly drove off the shoulder of the road and the next thing he remembered was the loud noise on the driver's side of his car as he careened down the side of a steep hill. The ride down the hill seemed to last forever as his car hit a tree on the way down.

His eyes hurt as the bright hospital room lights shone on his face. He did not recognize any of the people in the room other than the tear stained face of Anna. She stood at his bedside with her hand squeezing his. He had been deliberately driven off the road by someone who was obviously trying to injure or kill him. He was knocked unconscious when his head was slammed against the steering wheel.

Other than bumps and minor bruises he was fine and was not seriously injured. The doctor said he was very lucky because he was wearing his seatbelt, which prevented him from flying through the windshield head first.

"Who would do something like this, Mark?" Anna asked.

"I don't know, sweetheart, but they were not successful and I'm alive and thankful to God that you and the baby are still in my life," he replied as he began to tear up. Anna looked at his swollen, bruised face and wept as she looked at the man that she knew was her true love.

Mark did not go back to work for a few weeks while he recuperated at home. Anna would not take her eyes off him as she took care of him. Mark spent hours thinking about his relationship with Anna and how quickly things could change in the flicker of an eye. Anna sat by the bed while he sipped her homemade chicken noodle soup. She was expecting him to comment on the soup, since it was his favorite. Instead he looked at her and asked,

"Will you marry me, Anna?"

She remained silent and stared. "Do you truly understand what you just asked me, Mark?"

"Yes, I do."

"Mark, I have loved you since the first night we spent together at Danny's beach house. After that night I was so afraid and confused because the feelings I felt were nothing like the feelings I had for my husband. I did not want to see you again because I did not trust myself when I was with you. I loved my husband, but with you it was a type of love I had never known and did not understand. The only thing I knew was that somehow I wanted to be with you, but I had resigned myself to the fact that it was impossible because of the situation at that time." He listened carefully as she spoke and asked again.

"Will you marry me?"

"YES! I will. This is the happiest day in my life. I don't want to be overly dramatic, but I feel reborn, Mark," she told him as they embraced.

"Ouch! Mark yelped

"What's wrong?"

"You are hurting me...I'm still sore from the accident."

They giggled with delight.

The police told Mark they had a possible lead on the car that tried to run him off the road and they would be in touch soon. Anna was confident that the cops would locate the fool who tried to hurt Mark. She focused on staying healthy and taking care of Mark. Soon he was back at work and all was well. He had not heard from Merritt and was no longer being followed, as far as he could tell.

Mark called Anna and told her he would pick her up later and to change her clothes to something a little dressy but not formal. "Why do you want me to change my clothes, honey?"

"We need to take care of something today."

"Ok, but why the big mystery?"

'See ya soon, Anna, bye."

She was amused, but mostly curious. L.A. traffic was a nightmare and Anna wondered why in the world would Mark travel downtown this time of day right before the daily commute. She was a little perplexed until she entered the parking garage at City Hall. Mark had been unusually quiet up until that point.

He grabbed her by the hand as they entered the building and the hallway was filled with people who were standing and smiling as soon as they walked in. Someone yelled, "Here they come," as a tall guy with a red beard gave her a wet kiss on the cheeks and congratulated her.

"What's going on?" she said laughingly.

Mark had arranged for some of his closest friends and colleagues to meet him at City Hall and witness the marriage of Anna Cain to Mark Swiser. Anna was shocked and overjoyed. She was not expecting this on a slow Wednesday afternoon in downtown L.A. "I don't have a ring, Mark." Before the words left her lips he slipped the largest diamond ring she had ever seen on her finger. The Justice of the Peace who conducted the ceremony was one of Mark's close friends, and when he finished he broke out in tears and everyone laughed. Anna and Mark laughed and cried. This was the best afternoon surprise Anna had ever experienced.

They held a private reception on Laguna Beach at sunset with close friends. Six weeks later, a new life entered the world at UCLA Medical Center. Evan Frederic Swiser was born on January 10, 2014, at a healthy nine pounds six ounces. He was born on the same day as her former husband Evan, who would have turned 30 years old on January 10. Mark fainted when he laid eyes on his son for the first time.

Weeks later Anna received a long distance call from a Mr. Pierre from Athens, Greece. She did not know anyone by that name, but returned his call because he left a message stating the purpose of his call was highly confidential.

"Hello, Mrs. Bulon."

"Yes, this is Anna Swiser, formerly Anna Bulon."

"My name is Henri Pierre and I am the custodian of the late Simone Sason's estate. I will need certain personal information from you in order to have your funds transferred by wire to your personal account in America."

"What funds? What are you talking about?"

"The late Madame Simone Sason's estate stipulated that certain funds be forwarded to you in the case of her death."

"What!"

"Yes, Mrs. Swiser, you have $3,456,654 dollars that is scheduled for transfer on February 15 and we need you to identify a financial institution so we can transfer the funds to your account."

Anna felt faint and reeled slightly on her feet as she tried to allow what she just heard to sink in.

"Are you still there, Mrs. Swiser?"

"Yes I'm fine, just a little overwhelmed."

He requested a few more personal details and said he would be in touch soon. She literally fell to the floor as the phone fell from her hand. She could not stop laughing and finally screamed in joy. "I CANNOT FUCKING BELIEVE THIS!" Simone had designated Anna as one of three beneficiaries who would receive certain funds from her estate in the event of her death. Anna was still in shock as she called her bank in San Francisco to inquire about her current balance. She was overdrawn by $13.45.

About the Author

Sonny B. Allen is a California writer based in the San Francisco Bay Area. In the past several years he has dedicated himself to publishing stories that he considers original and engaging.